Quick Feng Shui Cures

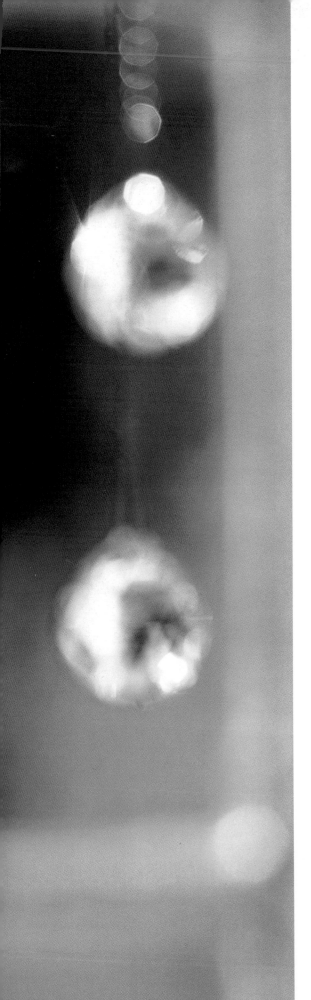

Quick Feng Shui Cures

Simple solutions
and secret tips
for a healthy, happy
and successful life

Text by
SARAH SHURETY

from the Editors of **HEALTHY LIVING** Magazine

Hearst Books
New York

Sometimes you meet really special people
and from now and for all eternity I wish for
everything good in the world for:
Colin Broster; Leigh, Sean, Dominic and
Brian Blaquiere; Sara, Peter, Daniel, James
and Ben Huntingdon; Karin Parkhouse;
Jane Nottage; Rowland Chute; Peter Saunders;
David Tomlin; Nin, Jo and Terry Williams;
Katrina Tremlett; Elizabeth Williams;
Tim Ramsay; Emily Tremlett; the Dixes; my dear
uncle Steve; Deanne; all the Shurety family; my
hard working father; and last, but not least,
Justin Lusty!
These names are written in no order of priority.

A special thank you to Grant Feller,
Cherry Maslem and Nicky Thompson
for their wonderful support.

To those of you who have invited me into your
homes and shared some of your life during feng
shui consultations, those who have studied with
me and every reader of this book I wish you a
long, healthy life and happiness.

Text copyright © 1999 by Sarah Shurety

Sarah Shurety has asserted her right to be identified as the author of this work
in accordance with the Copyright, Designs and Patents Act, 1988.

It is the policy of William Morrow and Company, Inc., and its imprints and
affiliates, recognizing the importance of preserving what has been written, to
print the books we publish on acid-free paper, and we exert our best efforts to
that end.

Library of Congress Cataloging-in-Publication Data

Shurety, Sarah.
Quick feng shui cures for your home/ Sarah Shurety:
editors of Country living healthy living.
p.   cm.
ISBN 0-688-17297-0
1. Feng Shui. I. Country living's Healthy living. II. Title.
BF 1779. F4S5635 2000
133.3'337-- dc21

Designed by Lovelock & Co.
Edited by Nicky Thompson
Special photography by Colin Walton
Picture research and styling by Emily Hedges
Index by Hilary Bird

Printed and bound in Italy by L.E.G.O.s.p.a.

1 2 3 4 5 6 7 8 9 10

www.williammorrow.com
www.healthyliving.com

Contents

Part One: feng shui concepts

Feng shui has been studied and practiced for thousands of years but it is only relatively recently that people in the Western world have turned to this ancient art to find solutions that will ease all aspects of their lives. The key to feng shui is that everything should be in balance and harmony. But before you can apply feng shui cures to rectify or improve any imbalances, you need to understand the basic concepts of feng shui and discover how everything is related. This section of the book explains these basic feng shui principles, and makes them easy to understand.

After a brief history of feng shui, you will find suggestions on how best to use this book. This is followed by an explanation of chi (the energy which surrounds all things), including what can happen when it moves too quickly or too slowly. Then there is all you need to know about the bagua (a flexible template with which you can identify the different areas in your home and how they relate to corresponding aspects of your life); the five elements theory; and the ten classic cures on which the specific cures in Part Two are based. Finally, there is advice on how to cleanse your home.

Introduction

"Has he luck?" was the first question that the Emperor Napoleon asked of any likely associate, while the fabulously wealthy Rothschilds said, "Never have anything to do with an unlucky place." It is easy to understand and agree with these sentiments, and the good news is that with the application of feng shui it is possible to improve anyone's luck.

Feng shui originated in China more than 3,000 years ago, so it has well and truly withstood the test of time. Its principal aim is to improve every aspect of life—including finances, relationships and health—by creating balance and harmony in the environment. *Feng* means wind, which is an analogy for health, and *shui* means water—which is another way of saying wealth of mind, body and spirit.

The law of perpetual motion

There is a great deal of contradiction and confusion over feng shui which can be very frustrating for the serious student. One of the reasons for this is the law of predecessor chi (*chi* means energy). The law is simply that if you repeat an action a sufficient number of times it becomes self-perpetuating. According to legend, this law (with respect to feng shui) was set in motion by a peasant named Yu Yang Chang. Although he was very poor, he was bright and one day he came across a manuscript of classical feng shui. He studied it carefully and, deciding that he had nothing to lose, moved his meager belongings from a cave where he was living to another site with favorable feng shui. He followed the advice and when the time was right he joined the Chinese army. After a short time he rose through the ranks and became a general—quite a feat in itself. He then continued his meteoric rise until he finally became Emperor of China, a truly extraordinary accomplishment. (Incidentally, by using feng shui, he also predicted the date and method of his downfall.)

Yu Yang Chang then apparently changed his name to Wen. Almost as soon as he took up this powerful role he called all the feng shui masters together and, realizing that feng shui had helped to put him in this position, he reserved the best feng shui masters for his sole use for the good of the country. He believed that the Emperor is the "captain of the ship" (if his energy is balanced he will steer the ship on a good course, if he is not in balance he might steer the whole country off course).

Emperor Wen then decreed that all the other masters should go out and start to spread red herrings about feng shui to create confusion about the subject and thus decrease the chances of anyone using feng shui to plot his demise (feng shui can be used for good or bad purposes). To this day, by the law of "predecessor chi," that confusion remains. But this has resulted in some advantages as well as disadvantages. On the one hand feng shui can be confusing and frustrating, full of contradictions, but on the other it is like a fascinating cryptic crossword that has to be deciphered. To understand feng shui fully you have to use and study it practically, check what your data tells you and draw your own conclusions. This is one of the reasons why to be a master you need to apply practical applications and witness events for 81 years (the length of time it takes to complete one cycle).

The applications of feng shui

Feng shui can be applied to a country, your home, your handbag, virtually anything. One of its first applications was to establish the most auspicious dates for funerals and the placement of graves. The Chinese heed the expression "The sins of the father will be visited on the son for the next seven generations," and therefore always seek to keep their ancestors, past and present, happy.

Feng shui is the art of working out and influencing someone's destiny. To do this, you need to make a detailed study of his or her date and place of birth, the five elements and the environment in which they live.

Everything in this universe works in cycles of expansion and contraction, whether it be climatic changes relating to the planet or the lifespan of a person or even something like a business. For instance, there will be a time when a business is expanding very rapidly, times of contraction and inevitably its demise or metamorphosis and rebirth into something different. Feng shui can accurately predict a business's or a person's fate, and suggest when life, death, riches, honor, failure, poverty or even love are likely to occur.

Chinese and Japanese astrology are used to read someone's destiny, inviting the logical question that if two people are born at exactly the same time, surely according to astrology they should have the same personality and destiny. The reason that this doesn't happen is not that astrology is inaccurate but that the environmental influence also has to be considered.

If you were a sunflower and you were planted in rich soil in a place where you receive lots of sunshine, rain and gentle wind, then you would grow into a big, beautiful and healthy

Choosing a property

Most people will have noticed a store in the local main street that keeps going into liquidation for no logical reason. The property next door is prospering and has been there for generations. The store seems to be in a good location but, no matter how different each new venture is, or how enthusiastic the new entrepreneurs, it seems destined for failure too. If you take over a property that has a history of bankruptcy or of failed relationships (perhaps you buy a property from a couple who are forced to sell because they are getting divorced, and they in turn originally bought from a couple in a similar situation), by the dictates of the predecessor law, the cycle is likely to keep repeating. The situation will not be remedied until the unfavorable feng shui is cured. So, when you are looking for new premises, enquire about the history. Try to choose a property where the previous occupants have prospered; this won't guarantee you the same success but it's a good start. (In Hong Kong house details come with a history and it is quite normal to ask about the previous occupants.)

sunflower. But supposing you were growing in exhausted, untilled soil and there was very little rain and no sun, then you would not reach your potential. In the same way, a poor man, with little food (emotional, spiritual and physical) and shelter will not reach the same potential as a rich man with lots of "food" and good shelter.

In a corresponding way, our destiny is influenced by the site and the shape of buildings. Feng shui masters have noticed after thousands of years of observation that, for example, someone living in a large dome-shaped building is likely to attract spiritual and material wealth, whereas someone living in an L-shaped house is destined to live a lonely existence.

The date someone moves into a building, the date the building was constructed, the shape of the building, the immediate environment and the direction from which we have moved can make the difference between success and failure.

In brief there are four principal aspects to feng shui:

1 The external environment that is influencing you.

2 The internal geography within your building.

3 Timing—including planning an activity at the right time. According to feng shui, the date that you start a business or the date you marry will have a significant impact on your success.

4 Direction. The world is swathed in magnetic belts called the Van Allen belts that run from the North to the South Pole. They significantly influence us because at the heart of every cell is iron, and iron is very sensitive to magnetism.

Every time we make a significant move our personal energy is influenced. This explains why you can go on vacation and have a fantastic time, but you could return six months later to exactly the same location and be strangely disappointed. You don't meet anyone, you lose things and you feel tired. This is because you have moved in a direction at a time that has taken your energy away. There is a multitude of different influences—some good, some detrimental.

When you go on vacation you might go for a weekend or a couple of weeks, and the influence lasts for a short period of time, usually for about a month. But when you move house, as long as the distance is more than one and a half miles, the influence can last from three to 20 years, giving you a good luck period or some learning experiences. So you need to move in the right direction at the right time (for your best directions, see pages 48–49).

External wind chimes are usually hung from a tree, but if this is not viable, you can also hang one from your home to improve the surrounding chi.

How to use this book

The journey you are about to begin, by reading this book and applying some of its feng shui cures, will lead you to make positive changes to your life.

One of the most important things to remember is that you should never underestimate the influence our homes have upon us. If you live in a dark and dank basement apartment with bars on every window, this will influence you on a deeply physical and psychological level. Your house is your home and should be your protector, not your adversary. The aim of this book is to give you a series of quick cures that will help to make this a reality.

Drawing upon my extensive experience of feng shui consultations, I have tried to translate Far-Eastern secrets so that they are relevant to contemporary issues. You don't always have to make big changes to balance unfavorable feng shui; often the cure is quite subtle and involves little effort. For example, if you are undergoing financial problems, simply hanging a framed mirror near your front door in the appropriate location can be sufficient. This book of cures is a gallery of remedies; you can use it as a reference book to be dipped into from time to time, or you can apply as many cures as are necessary as you progressively sort out each area of your home or life. The best ways to use this book are:

1 To identify which areas of your home relate to which aspects of your life.

2 To find out how to solve a specific problem within your life by using a feng shui cure.

3 To use feng shui to make a special event like a wedding, christening, Christmas gathering or even a dinner party go really well.

4 To solve problems relating to your career, relationships, family, health, friends, children, study and your future.

5 To select cures. If you are not in a position to make major structural changes to your home, you can use this book to select a temporary feng shui cure to keep you going. Please note, however, that some of these cures are designed to "tweak" an area and if there is a major problem they may not be sufficient to heal it completely.

When I first came across feng shui, I was skeptical but open. However, I followed its principles and it improved my life dramatically. In particular, I discovered that choosing the right home and moving in the right direction at the right time has had a monumentally positive effect on my health, happiness and finances. So has using many of the cures in this book. Feng shui can do the same for you.

Keeping your balance

One of the priorities of feng shui is to make sure that chi (energy) flows smoothly. If it flows too fast it will make us feel pressured and therefore likely to act impetuously and possibly in a dangerous way. By contrast, if we are in an area where energy is moving too slowly it can create stagnation which, according to my dictionary, means "without current, foul, unwholesome or dull from stillness." If there is stagnation, illness can develop.

Energy moving too fast

Westerners first discovered feng shui when they became involved in the laying of the railroad tracks in China. As each section was completed and congratulations and admiration were sought, it was with surprise that the engineers noted that the villagers were not happy. Instead, they said "You've cut the dragon's veins; it's the beginning of the end." What had happened was that very straight, long railroads had been laid right through the center of the villages, effectively cutting each community into two areas.

In the language of feng shui we refer to roads, paths or railroad tracks as "rivers" because they are all thoroughfares; things move upon them and they convey movement. These Chinese villages with their dividing railroads can be compared to any major city like London that has a clear division; the people who live north of the Thames wouldn't want to live south and vice versa. It follows then, that any small town or suburb that has an expressway, railroad tracks or river running through its center will share the following influences:

1 Neighbors on opposite sides of a street have little to do with each other because the road divides their "community."

2 The "river" will flow fast, and cars will travel at speed. Drivers won't be able to stop at stores edging the road because by the time they have seen them, they have driven past and it's too late—and so businesses will start to die.

3 Children and animals are more likely to be run over by traffic.

4 The suburb or small town no longer has a heart so everything starts to take place around the edges. For example, if there is a park in the center of the town children will play there; if there isn't they may play out of sight down quiet back alleys, which can lead to undesirable behavior. When things are done covertly, especially by young people who are testing the boundaries of life, crime is likely to rise.

On a larger scale, if you consider some modern cities in America and Australia, you will find that they are built on a grid system of fast-flowing "rivers," which divide the city many times into many different communities. There is no central heart so things happen around the edges. Also, you can be happily window shopping in one street, where it is warm and still, then you can walk round a corner and almost get knocked off your feet by a gust of wind. This unsettles our energy and makes us do things we would not normally do. We can become irritable. Most people are innately good at heart but, when they are in an unbalanced environment, they feel pressured. This in turn can lead to an increase in crime. Because New York is a sprawling concrete city with tall skyscrapers, the changes in energy are extreme and so we can expect everything there to be extreme.

Amsterdam in Holland is also built on a grid system that divides the city many times, but its "rivers" are mainly created by a grid of canals. Water influences our kidneys and is associated with sex and drugs so we can expect the negative energies that build up to be linked to these activities. To those who study feng shui, it comes as no surprise that Amsterdam has thriving pornography and drug industries.

In comparison, in a small country town, the roads are more meandering so chi moves more slowly, in a healthy way. There may be a pond, a park, perhaps a post office, a bar and a store. These all give the town a heart and a clearly defined center. Now things will tend to happen in the open; crime cannot survive in this environment because people are more relaxed and therefore more civil to each other. In this environment those who start to stress their nervous systems by taking drugs or working too hard will find that they will not be happy and so they will move to somewhere like a city which has more "tension." Any crimes in towns are generally perpetrated by people who come from another area that has these fast-flowing "rivers."

We sometimes create these dangerously fast-flowing "rivers" in microcosm in our own homes. For example, when we have a front door lined up with a back door, we have created a little river that flows straight in and straight out of the property very quickly. It energetically divides the house and this can result in stress and tension because there are two sides to the house. Apparently, Prince Andrew and the Duchess of York moved into a house that had a long corridor leading from the front door to the back. Sarah's quarters were on one side of this corridor and Andrew's were on the other, which perhaps unintentionally contributed to the breakdown of their marriage.

Feng shui case study

Two of my clients, a delightful couple living in a palatial house, invited me to give them a consultation. They had hit upon hard times, finances were not good, they were not getting on well, they were sleeping badly and the husband had developed asthma. When I looked around their home I discovered that their bedroom was above a swimming pool (which was in the wealth area of the first floor). It was stagnant, in a sorry state of neglect and had green algae growing in the water. Because the pool was below the bedroom, it was having a significant influence on their marriage, making it stale and lending a sinking quality to their health, finances and relationship.

I recommended that renovating the pool was one of the most important things they should do. They thought I was mad because it seemed senseless to spend so much money on the pool when their financial situation was so dire. However, they decided to follow my advice anyway and within three months their finances had recovered. Most importantly, so had their health and their relationship.

Energy moving too slowly

When we build a home in a basement, or we have rooms with no windows or even with north-facing windows, or skylights that will not open, we automatically create stagnation and in this environment disease can breed. You only have to look at a stagnant pond to see that it is an environment where disease proliferates. Mosquitoes breed there and during the hot summer months the water can become fetid and odorous, simply because there is no movement.

Traditionally, houses were built around a courtyard so that there was plenty of free-flowing air and all rooms had direct daylight. Increasingly, however, we are building houses with bathrooms or toilets in the center of the house and in our townhouses we are building extensions at the back, making a middle room with no direct daylight. This creates an environment in which we become subtly less healthy.

Feng shui case study

I have a lovely client who used to live in a sweet London mews house. When I visited her, it was almost impossible to move in her home because it was filled to the brim with possessions and antique furniture. It was a real Aladdin's cave, but there was no room to move. After living there for ten years and accumulating all these possessions, my client never invited anyone to her home and rarely went out, work had dried up and she was depressed. She wanted to go home to America but could not summon the energy. It did not take a budding Einstein to work out what had happened. The clutter had completely taken over. She is very bright and was willing to change so while I was there she arranged for an auction house to do a valuation. Later, they sold most of her possessions, which enabled her to return to her homeland. She very quickly met a wonderful man and has regained her charming, sociable and outgoing self.

The moral is that this lovely, talented lady started off just collecting a few bits and pieces and then things got out of control. Don't let this happen to you.

Clearing out clutter

When we fill our homes with endless paraphernalia we start to congest our environment still further. Feng shui endorses the motto "less is more." As we fill our homes with books, ornaments, china for best and for everyday use, and perhaps two teakettles (one for emergencies) we slow down movement.

When we have too many things we find we spend all our time trying to keep our belongings in some semblance of order. Instead of going out and meeting people and having fun, we spend all our time tidying our homes, which often involves making piles of things and moving them from one place to another. We don't invite people over for dinner because we are embarrassed about our chaotic, overstuffed homes.

In addition, we work inordinately hard so we can afford to fill our homes with too many things. In fact, some people do not move house simply because they cannot bear the thought of packing. Having too many belongings can make us ill and depressed. The more possessions you have, the more insecure you become. Keep a happy balance. Remember that shopping can be great fun but keep it in perspective. Whenever I buy something new I throw something away. If you have a lot of clutter at the moment then you could discard two old items for every one thing that comes into your house.

Tips for de-cluttering

1 Take a few minutes to go through each room in your home and work out what percentage of each area is filled with disorganized piles of things that don't really have a home. This should inspire you to begin letting things go.

2 Get three boxes, and name them Trash, Presents and Returns. Fill Trash with anything that is past its sell-by date. Into Presents put articles you can pass on to friends and family as gifts (don't wait until Christmas or birthdays—give them immediately). Returns is for items you have been storing for friends or family (give them a date for collection). Remember, too, that many charity stores welcome good-quality rejects. Start filling up those boxes!

3 When you are deciding whether to retain or recycle something, see if you feel a lift in your energy when you touch it. If you don't, you know what to do with it!

4 Start small—perhaps with a kitchen drawer. It can be quite overwhelming to tackle emptying something large, whereas if you start with a small space or area you see the results quickly.

5 Pile things up in your hall. You will get so fed up with trampling over them it will be easy to let them go. I used this technique when I was getting rid of a lot of books that I hadn't touched for years. They were getting dusty and tired and were just creating a blocked area but it had been so instilled into me from a young age that books are very special and must be treated with respect that I was finding it difficult. Eventually I took down most of the shelves in my living room, redecorated and didn't put back the shelves. I sorted through my books, took out reference material and books that I really loved, returned those to the few bookshelves that remained and piled all the rest up in my hallway. After a month of precarious piles falling over, and having to clean around them, I couldn't stand it, so I ferried them all to a charity store. That was over ten years ago and I haven't missed one. You can try this with clothes, kitchen utensils—almost everything.

6 Invite a friend to help you. Choose someone who understands the concept of space, so that they can be honest and easily say "that never suited you even though it cost a fortune," or "that is old and past it now," and help you to make space.

7 Imagine that you are moving house soon and ask yourself whether you really want to take all your possessions to the next property.

8 Move 27 things in your home that you usually keep in the same place, like a desk, a couch, or a television. Do this for nine consecutive days, so you start to get the energy moving around you. This combats the stagnation and encourages you into de-cluttering mode.

9 Thoroughly de-clutter one room at a time, so that you see the results more rapidly.

10 To help you to become organized, compartmentalize everything in your home from your wardrobe and chest of drawers in your bedroom to your handbag and kitchen cupboards and drawers.

11 Use a small wardrobe; the more space you have the more you fill it. If you give yourself little room you will soon get irritated with trying to squash things into the space. The answer is to cull your clothes!

12 Listen to lively music while you de-clutter to make you more active and get you into the swing of it.

13 Talk about the benefits of having fewer possessions to your friends until you feel inspired.

14 Throw away anything that is cracked or broken.

15 Adopt the Chinese habit of spring cleaning for the 15 days leading up to the New Year.

16 Invite friends over regularly so you get into the habit of clearing up for their arrival.

17 Adopt these maxims: "Something in, something out," and "Less is more."

Take your time. It takes years to accumulate clutter and only a few people manage to get everything into balance immediately. De-clutter one step at a time and try to incorporate the whole philosophy into your life. Most importantly, try to enjoy the process.

The bagua

According to feng shui, there are nine principal aspects of our lives that access different facets of our personalities, and if we are to be happy and successful there must be a good balance in each area. Not surprisingly, if we concentrate too much on one aspect of our lives, the balance in the others is upset and everything becomes out of kilter. Each aspect directly corresponds to a different area of our homes which is identified by a bagua template. Once you have learned how the bagua relates to your life and your home, you can apply feng shui cures to redress any imbalances.

The bagua is a template or map that shows how chi (energy) flows in our lives. Although bagua means eight houses, we actually have nine areas in our homes. The ninth corresponds to health and traditionally this was an open space with plenty of ventilation. It is surrounded by the other eight areas. The aspects of our lives and their corresponding numbers and bagua areas are as follows:

4 Wealth *wood dark green*	9 Fame *purple fire*	2 Relationship *black earth*
3 Ancestors *wood bright green*	5 Health *yellow earth*	7 Children *red (gold) metal*
8 Knowledge *white prasin earth*	1 Career *white water*	6 Helpful People *white metal*

The bagua is a flexible template which enables you to identify which parts of your home affect which aspects of your life, so you can apply feng shui to improve any imbalances. You can also apply the bagua to rooms or to your garden (position it so that the entrance that you use most frequently to the garden is the "front door").

1 Our day-to-day duties (career area).

2 One-to-one relationships (relationship area).

3 Family dynamics (ancestors area).

4 Financial situation and self-empowerment (wealth area).

5 Health of mind and body (health area).

6 Friendships (helpful people or benefactors area).

7 Our relationships with our children or things weaker than ourselves and hobbies (children area).

8 Learning and study (knowledge area).

9 Plans for the future (fame area).

Each different area of our environment, whether our home, office, a room or even a town, relates to an area of the bagua. To apply feng shui to your home, first you need to create a bagua template and use it to identify these areas. It is easiest to use a square bagua template and "stretch" this into a rectangle as required. You may already have an architect's plan of your home, but if not, draw the outline of your home, including all the doors and windows. Think of the bagua as a flexible template and physically or mentally lay it over your plan so that your front door is in the career area, helpful people area or knowledge area. Your front door is your main entrance—the mouth of chi—which is the door which people would naturally be drawn to if they had never been to your building before, and is where your mail is delivered.

Once you have completed this first stage, you can quickly see which areas other parts of your home relate to. Very few buildings are square, so extend and "stretch" the bagua to fit over the plan of your property.

4 Wealth	9 Fame	2 Relationship
3 Ancestors	5 Health	7 Children
8 Knowledge	1 Career	6 Helpful People

When you lay the bagua template over a plan of your home, make sure that the front door is in the area relating to knowledge, career or helpful people.

If you live in an upstairs apartment, think of the top stair as your front door and "draw" the line of the template back to align with the apartment's outside wall. You will probably find that one or two or more areas are either missing or extended. Do not be too worried about this. The cures in Part Two, which relate directly to each area of your life, will help to remedy the situation.

The five element theory

In addition to the bagua, feng shui also employs the use of the five element theory. All ancient Chinese disciplines share this simple fundamental philosophy. It supplies invaluable clues which help us to identify imbalances and select appropriate cures. The theory is based upon the five elements: water, wood, fire, earth and metal.

The tortoise or turtle has a water energy, but he also symbolizes the universe. His feet swim through water, his belly can be compared to the earth, his back represents the skies, and his shell (from which the bagua derives) mirrors the stars and planets.

Each of the areas within our home corresponds to one of these elements and you need to understand the theory so that you can identify the basic energy within a specific area and select cures that balance, harmonize and energize easily. Without an understanding of the five elements you will only be able to use cures that you have learned by rote. But with knowledge of the five elements, you can select the best way to balance the energy intelligently. Everything in the universe is identified with one of the five elements which describes and matches its basic make-up. Considering the basic natures of a cat, dog, tortoise, a rooster, and donkey helps to explain why they are placed in a particular category.

A young cat belongs to the tree (or wood) element. More specifically, it is that of a mature tree, which corresponds to late spring—the time when plants are in bud and new

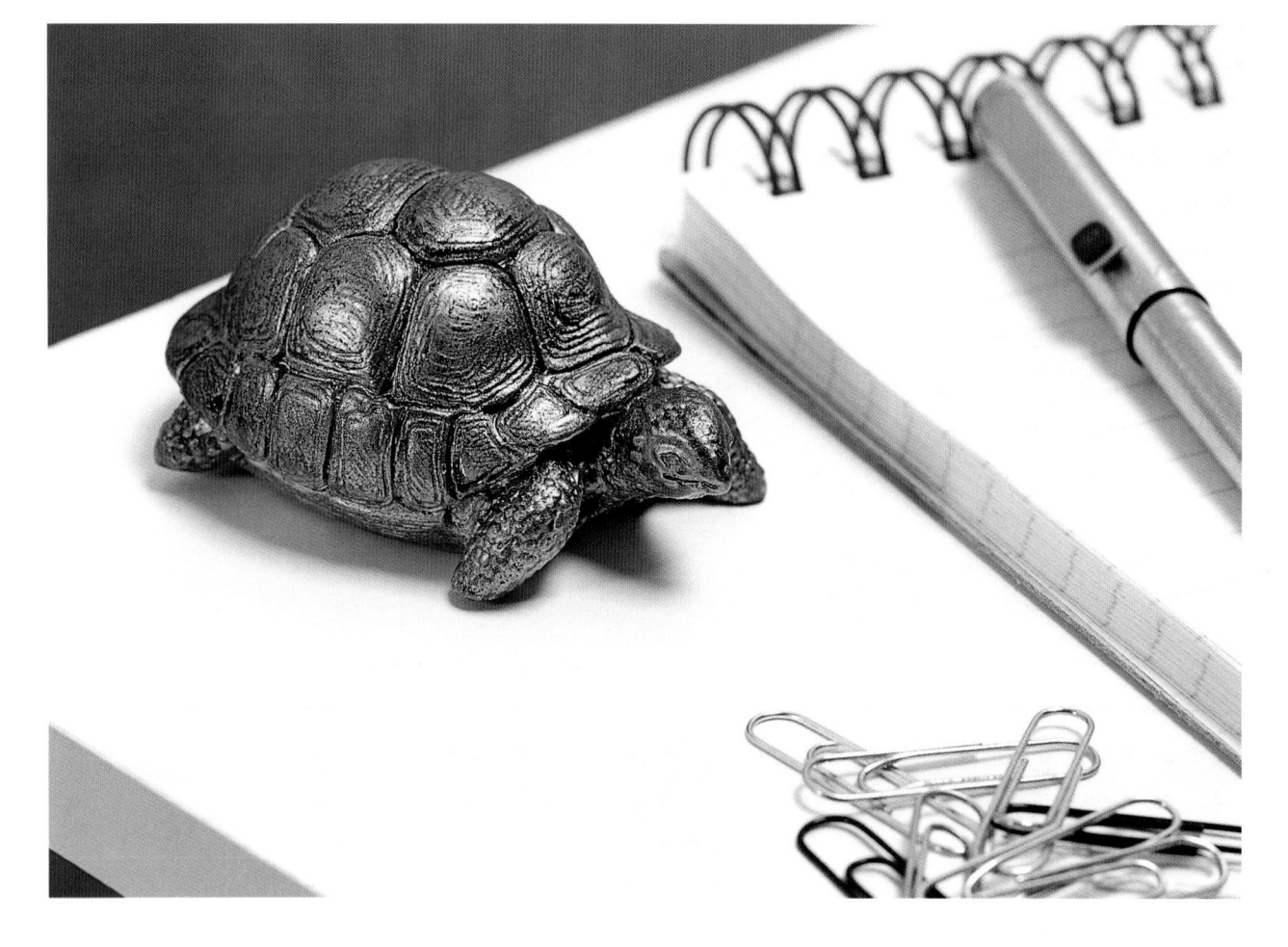

sprigs are growing. So the cat is curious by nature; it does not like routine; it prefers several sleeping places; it eats at different times of the day, and prefers to come and go as it pleases. It is impossible to restrict the growth of spring and, in the same way, a plant's natural inclination is to grow upwards. And even a small shoot can have the energy to crack a paving slab if its upward path is blocked. It cannot be trained; similarly, it is very difficult to teach a cat to perform tricks. To support the cat we need to understand its basic nature.

A dog belongs to the earth element. Earth corresponds to the energy of a mother and late summer. Everything is fairly still, balanced, and encouraging prosperity. There is little movement; the soil is rich, the wind gentle and conservative. A dog's nature is also conservative, it likes routine, it likes to sleep in the same place and to know what it can and can't do, and to eat at the same times. The dog is generally nurturing, faithful and true.

A crystal rooster. See pages 88–91 to find out your zodiac animal according to the Chinese horoscope.

A tortoise belongs to the water element, which relates to winter. It is steady and slow; the atmosphere is damp and dissolving and everything is slightly hidden. A tortoise's nature is secretive and determined.

A rooster belongs to the fire element. Fire corresponds to full summer when everything is in full bloom and at its most expansive. A fire will attract people to gather closely round it. It has a bright light and so the element is attributed with clarity and life-giving qualities. The rooster correspondingly struts around and calls attention to himself as he looks after his hens with great pride.

A donkey belongs to the metal element, which is linked to autumn. This is a time of contraction and withdrawal, when leaves are turning golden and starting to fall. Donkeys are melancholic, steady, intuitive and refined. They are also stubbornly determined.

Within these categories there will nearly always be sub-categories. One tortoise, for example, may stand out when compared to its contemporaries as being really fast and impetuous, displaying tree, or wood, tendencies. So although something has an overall water element, it may have qualities of the other four elements.

The qualities of the elements

Water: winter, stubborn, diplomatic, secretive, slow and sure.

Wood (or tree) _spring_: initiating, fast moving, open, not routine, curious, changeable.

Fire: _summer_ bright, clarifying, a need to be appreciated, egotistical, expansive.

Earth: nurturing, warm, maternal, grounded, steady, conservative.

Metal: _autumn_ rigid, refined, intuitive, completing, organized, depressed.

All the elements and various colors are linked with an area of the bagua as follows:

CAREER AREA: white water element

RELATIONSHIP AREA: black earth element

ANCESTORS AREA: bright green tree (or wood) element

WEALTH AREA: dark green tree (or wood) element

HEALTH AREA: yellow earth element

HELPFUL PEOPLE AREA: white metal element

CHILDREN AREA: red (gold) metal element

KNOWLEDGE AREA: white (porcelain) earth element

FAME AREA: purple fire element

In order to apply cures to each area in your home, you need to understand how to "feed" these elements to create more energy.

The creative cycle

This cycle works in a positive way to energize a particular area:

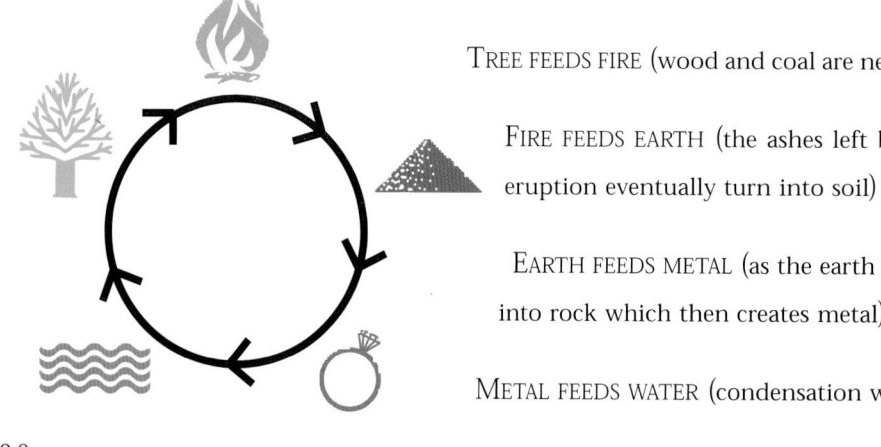

WATER FEEDS TREE (a plant cannot survive without water)

TREE FEEDS FIRE (wood and coal are necessary fuel for a fire to survive)

FIRE FEEDS EARTH (the ashes left behind after a fire or a volcanic eruption eventually turn into soil)

EARTH FEEDS METAL (as the earth is compressed over time it turns into rock which then creates metal)

METAL FEEDS WATER (condensation will be created on metal or glass)

Basic energizing tips

- If you want to energize your wealth area (which is wood) it would be good to use something that has a water element like a fish tank, a tortoise, a fountain, a picture of water or a blue carpet—anything that conjures up a feeling of water.

- If you need to increase the energy in your career area (water) you could add a cure from the metal element; it could be something white, metal furniture, wind chimes or a mirror.

- In the fame area (fire) you need something with a wood element, so placing a jade plant or a wooden object would be helpful.

- The health area (earth) needs to be energized with the fire element, so you could add a bright light or something in the shape of a pyramid.

- The helpful people area (metal) will be energized by the earth element, so you could put a Buddha there or a statue made of stone.

- In the children area (metal) you could hang a yellow framed square mirror. The square and yellow both belong to the earth element and the mirror to the metal. Since earth supports metal, and the mirror is surrounded by the earth, this is a very good cure.

The destructive cycle

As well as a creative cycle there is a destructive cycle that works as follows:

WATER PUTS OUT FIRE

FIRE MELTS METAL

METAL CUTS DOWN TREE

TREE EXHAUSTS EARTH (as a plant grows out of a flowerpot the soil becomes very tired)

EARTH MUDDIES WATER (just a sprinkling of soil can contaminate a whole glass of water)

Most feng shui practitioners generally avoid using items in areas where they are destructive. For example, it would be best not to place an indoor fountain (water) in the fame (fire) area.

Classic cures

The cures suggested here can be used to strengthen or redirect the chi (energy) flowing through your home—or slow it down if necessary. Many of the cures will also help to absorb shas (the name given to threatening elements). If you have a minor problem, it may be rectified with a very simple cure like hanging a bagua mirror in your hall or putting a healthy plant next to your computer. In most instances, however, a combination of cures will probably be more effective. This is a general introduction to cures. You will find the solutions to specific problems and the best uses for individual cures in Part Two.

Mirrors

Mirrors are often referred to as the aspirin of feng shui. They are very powerful and can energize a room effectively. For example, if you have a dark narrow room with a window looking out on to a rural area on one of the longer walls, by hanging a mirror opposite that

Ideally, mirrors should be framed. However, if you really want to hang unframed mirrors, always choose ones that have bevelled edges.

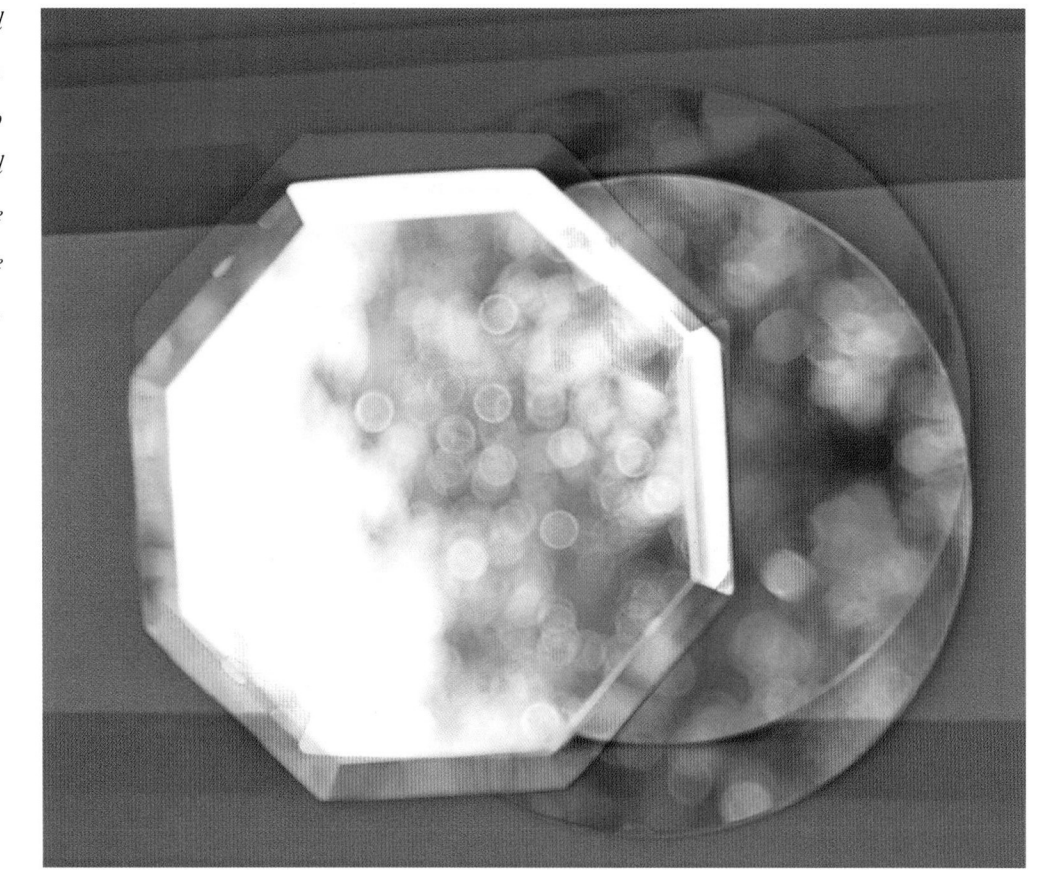

window you will draw in more light and expand the room so it appears more square than rectangular. This will energetically change the room 100 percent. If you have a missing area, perhaps because your house or apartment is L-shaped, then hanging a mirror on either wall that borders the missing area will create the illusion of space and help to balance the missing area.

Points to remember

- The bigger the better. When hanging mirrors you should be able to see the whole of your head and at least 5 inches above. We all have an energy field around us which reaches about an arm's length. This should be reflected in the mirror or you will subconsciously feel cramped.

- Whatever you reflect in a mirror, you draw into your home. If you are reflecting a busy road, you will be drawing a lot of fast-moving energy into your house which can create instability. On the other hand, if you are reflecting a beautiful tree in full blossom you will be adding a delicate soft energy into the house.

Choosing mirrors

Always use clean, good quality, new mirrors—although the frames may be antique. Similarly, steer well clear of tarnished or tinted mirrors or they will bring in tarnished energy. For instance, if they are hung in the wealth area you may be bringing in corrupt finances, and in the relationship area you may be inviting tainted relationships. It is also important to use mirrors that are either framed or bevelled, otherwise their sharp edges will send out a negative energy.

Bagua mirrors are the most powerful protective cure available. They comprise a small round mirror set within an octagonal frame inscribed with I Ching symbols. These are usually colored in an auspicious combination of red, gold and green and they act as runes. The mirror draws the negative energy towards it and the octagonal shape and the runes decorating the frame transmute any negative energy so that it is no longer harmful.

One of the most potent feng shui cures is to hang a bagua mirror so it transmutes any negative energy threatening your home.

Warnings about mirrors

- Throw away cracked or broken mirrors.
- Do not use mirrored tiles. When you look at an image reflected in mirrored tiles, it is all "cut up." This suggests to your subconscious mind that you have been cut into pieces. Over time this will create stress and will damage your health.
- Check that mirrors on dressing tables do not decapitate the user in any way and keep hand mirrors so that the mirror faces downwards.

Convex mirrors are the most powerful type of mirror. They absorb energy from all directions and expand it—thus making "big" things happen. In contrast, concave mirrors reduce energy so they can be used to slow down chi or to diminish a negative sha. If you place a mirror beside something so that it is reflected, you will double its energy.

Hanging mirrors

This may sound obvious, but always hang mirrors flat against a wall. Mirrors that hang forward give us a depressed perspective on life. Generally, you should never hang mirrors directly opposite each other or they will create an unstable environment. They will bounce energy backwards and forwards and create an uncomfortable atmosphere. The only exceptions to this are in a dining room, where mirrors opposite each other can encourage conversation to flow freely, and in a small bathroom, where mirrors can be used to create a feeling of space. If you are hanging mirrors in your bedroom, choose oval or round ones if possible. Avoid hanging a mirror so you can see your reflection while you are lying in bed. Otherwise, the mirror will draw your energy towards it and slow down the healing processes that naturally occur while you are asleep.

Crystals

Throughout history and all over the world, royalty and rulers have worn precious jewels like diamonds, emeralds and rubies to attract attention and draw energy towards themselves. Similarly, there is a long tradition for healers to use semi-precious crystals like amethyst and rose quartz to strengthen the power of their medicine. Few people are wealthy enough to use diamonds as a feng shui cure, but a practical and effective solution is to use the best quality crystal you can afford. This may be in the form of a hanging crystal, a chandelier, or simply a crystal ornament in the shape of an appropriate animal, bird or flower.

Using crystals

- Cleanse your crystals by holding them under cold running water before you use them in a cure. As you do this, imagine that any bad chi is being removed at the same time as physical dirt and dust.
- If you need to place a crystal ornament somewhere dark which receives little sunlight, sit it on a round, bevelled mirror to double its energy and strength.

The range of crystal cures

Crystals can be used in almost any area of the bagua to bring in the energy of refreshing light. Hanging crystals strengthen intuition and have the ability to change the flow of energy. They absorb chi and make it more intense. They can also prevent stagnation within an area by sending out myriad prisms that dapple the room and fill it with the moving energy of the sun. Use hanging crystals that are clear, faceted and spherical. I prefer to use high-quality Austrian crystal. Hang spherical crystals in a window using a piece of silver thread.

If you have a lot of stagnation in an area with no windows or with only a north window which receives little sunshine, then you can place a collection of cut crystal animals on a display mirror. The mirror will capture the light and empower the crystals. A crystal chandelier is also energized by light (fire energy). If you raise your head to look at the chandelier on a regular basis it will lift your energy. In fact, this very movement of looking up will raise your energy. When depressed, we usually slump our shoulders and take shallow breaths. If we sit up straight and breathe deeply, it is much more difficult to stay depressed. In the same way, anything that makes us look physically upwards subtly makes us much more inclined to be happy and cheerful in spirit.

A single, spherical, faceted crystal hung from a thread in a window will send dappled sunlight into a room and thus encourage positive chi to flow freely.

Lighting

All living things are naturally drawn towards light, so if you leave a light on in any area where you would like to see more activity it will be beneficial. This is a particularly effective cure to use in the relationship, knowledge or health area. Dim lighting can create headaches and depression, so bringing more light into your life is also likely to lead to an improvement in your health.

If a house is below the level of the road then a light just above the street will help to raise the levels of energy and opportunity. If a house is an awkward shape, perhaps L-shaped, it creates a missing area which leads to problems. A good cure is to install a floodlight outside in the garden and direct it to shine over the missing area. Turning the light on in the evening will help to correct the imbalance that has been caused by the missing area.

Right: keeping a lamp
on during the day lifts
the energy in a room
and can also help to
cure addictions.

Far right: before you
hang wind chimes in
the garden or inside,
check that you like the
noise it makes.

Useful sources of light

Like the flames in a fireplace, candles throw out a gentle and flattering light that warms the atmosphere and encourages people to gather around. As well as being a physical source of light, traditionally candles have been used on altars to represent a connection between the earthly and the spirit worlds or to represent eternal life. In recent years, candles have become a more fashionable choice for lighting and are not just reserved for the table during supper or dinner parties. You can use them anywhere in your home but especially wherever you want to encourage conversation.

Up-lights will help to raise energy and generally create a bright atmosphere. They are a vital form of lighting in basement apartments but can be useful in all situations. Not surprisingly, down-lights draw the light downwards which can help you feel more grounded if you live or work at the top of a tall building.

Tips on lighting

- Avoid burning black candles—for good feng shui choose paler colors like cream and pink.
- Remember that candles are a fire hazard. Never leave them unattended—and if you burn candles near plants or flowers, make sure they can't scorch them.
- Fluorescent tube lighting has been shown to cause frequent headaches and is a form of lighting you should avoid. If it is impossible for you to change this type of lighting in your workplace, use a task light on your desk.
- Up-lights should sit on or very close to the floor. Wall lights and tall, free-standing lamps that throw light upwards can cause problems. This is because the light they throw out is too close to the ceiling and is bounced off it.

Sounds

For hundreds of years shopkeepers in the Far East have used bells and wind chimes to protect their stores from thieves, and attract business from passers-by. So it is no surprise that sound has its role in feng shui. Most people are extremely sensitive to noise and all types of sound can energize us; a beautiful piece of music or a song can move us to tears, but a persistent burglar alarm or the sound of drilling can drive us to distraction.

Sound waves vibrate in the air and disturb the chi flowing through your rooms. Hanging wind chimes in the appropriate area of your home can help to cleanse the atmosphere and restore a balance. Most importantly, sound needs to be used with consideration. If you hang wind chimes from a tree in your garden, they may be giving you a great deal of pleasure. But if the same wind chimes are disturbing your neighbors so much that they cannot sleep, you may end up with them sending you serious negative psychological thoughts as they dream of doing

Choosing sounds

- Music can alter a room's atmosphere. If it is loud and cheerful, it will bring an uplifting energy—which is particularly encouraging if you are cleaning.
- Playing soothing sounds of nature can help to relax and inspire you.

despicable things to you and your wind chimes. This will be very bad for you and for them!

In your home, wind chimes hung so that they tinkle when a door opens or closes helps to remind you that you are moving from one area into another. In the same way, a bead curtain, which makes a much softer noise, can be hung to form a barrier between rooms. It will tell you when someone enters the room and can slow down the movement of chi.

Plants

Plants represent growth and they absorb negativity. They can help combat negative energy emitted by computers and to soak up noise pollution. In Chinese philosophy it is thought that if your plants are flourishing so is your health; if your plants are not doing well, then you are not taking sufficient care of yourself. Plants can become linked energetically to us. One of my teachers, Mr. Ng, has several rose trees growing in his garden. Each tree is "dedicated" to a person he really cares about and he knows how they are getting on simply by observing how the plant is prospering.

Most places within your home will benefit from plants, and the general rule is that the taller they are the better. Plants are growing things and so they subtly move the energy around your rooms. They also create a fresh chi within the area around them. Each different plant and type of flower has a different attribute. A spiky plant, like a cactus or a yucca, might be used near a vulnerable entrance to discourage intruders. A money (or jade) plant is associated with wealth and good fortune and will help to energize finances. Narcissi or daffodils will bring new beginnings and luck. A number of other plants, trees and flowers are listed as specific cures in Part Two.

Healthy plant tips

- Do not neglect your plants. Keep them healthy by giving them the right amount of water and gently wipe dust off their leaves.
- Cut flowers freshen the atmosphere.
- Remember that the life expectancy of artificial flowers is only six months, when you should either cleanse them thoroughly or replace them.

Living things

Animals give a wonderful warm earth energy to any area. Legend says that the cat is particularly lucky because in its youth it is attributed with the ability to see demons and chase them away. The black cat is most fortunate because it has the advantage of being able to see imps before they see him. The dog brings a lovely earth energy which is very warm, comforting and protective. Wherever the animal is sleeping will affect that area; wherever the animal happens to be will also have a positive influence, especially upon your health. Most offices would benefit from an animal even if it is just fish in a tank.

Fish are very good for finances and can be used practically anywhere within the home. I have two fish tanks and they have helped my financial situation enormously. Every time the fish outgrow their tanks, I put them in the pond. I think about not replacing them because they are so time consuming and such a responsibility, but I always notice a subtle drop in my finances until they are replaced! Dark fish protect your health, gold fish protect your finances and general luck.

Effective feng shui

- If you cannot live with a pet for some reason, ornaments and paintings of animals, birds and fish are effective feng shui cures.
- Remember that the color of ornaments, and the material from which they are made (wood, metal or crystal, for instance) will influence their energy and effectiveness as a cure.

Like all living things, and representations of creatures, birds are good feng shui. They move chi in your garden and bring more energy to your land. Mythological birds like the phoenix also have great powers and significance. You will find lots of specific cures that involve living and mythological creatures in Part Two.

For good feng shui, plants should be as tall as possible. Also, make sure they are not blocking doorways or the flow of traffic in your home.

Colors

Every color carries a different vibration and so the way we use color can subtly or dramatically change our lives. Color forms an integral part of our environment and its use is one of the most immediate and effective feng shui cures because color influences chi in the surrounding atmosphere. This is easier to understand if you think about how a room that is predominantly yellow or orange always feels warmer and more welcoming than one that is decorated in white, gray or blue.

Each color of the spectrum is thought of as representing certain qualities and is associated with one of the five elements. So taking color into consideration is very important when you are applying a cure. Many colors are described in more detail in the specific cures in Part Two. The meanings of different colored handbags are given on pages 102–103 and the influence of color on fashion is described on pages 132–133. Here are the intrinsic meanings of color and the areas of the bagua in which they are best used.

Black is associated with the water element and is good to use in the career, ancestors and wealth areas. It is a powerful, absorbing color that should be used with other colors. It also symbolizes money and wealth, but use it sparingly.

Blue is also associated with the water element and, like black, is appropriate for the career, ancestors and wealth areas. It represents faith, fidelity and consideration and is a calm, cooling color.

Brown is associated with the earth element and can be used in the knowledge, relationship and helpful people areas. It is a down-to-earth, solid color so it often represents practicality and reliability.

Green is associated with the tree element and is a good color for the wealth, ancestors and fame areas. Green brings tranquillity, peace and growth. It is often linked with travel and can imply jealousy, but it mainly symbolizes balance and harmony.

Gray is associated with the metal element and can be used in the career, helpful people and children areas. It can represent depression and fear, so you should avoid gray unless you are very confident and cheerful.

Orange is associated with the fire or the earth element (depending on the shade) and is good to use in the relationship, knowledge, health, helpful people and children areas.

Orange is a sociable color that gathers people together. It represents both mental and physical activity as well as joy.

Pink is associated with the fire and the earth elements and is best used in the relationship and knowledge areas. Pink is a warm, soothing color that represents health, healing and love. It is often used as a feng shui cure to encourage romance and happiness.

Purple is associated with the fire element and is a good color for the relationship, knowledge and fame areas. It is an auspicious color that has been linked for centuries with the church, nobility and power. It frequently symbolizes truth, love, high ideals and devotion.

Red is associated with the fire element. You should never use too much red but you can apply splashes of it in the relationship, knowledge and fame areas. Red is the color of blood, life and happiness, and is used extensively in celebrations by the Chinese who consider it the luckiest and most auspicious color. This is why they give red shirts to newborn babies and put lucky money in red envelopes.

Cheerful sunflowers mixed with sprays of goldenrod bring a touch of uplifting yellow to a room.

White is associated with the metal element and can be used in the children, helpful people and career areas. Traditionally, white is the Chinese color of mourning and is a non-color. It represents purity and new beginnings.

Yellow is associated with the earth element and is a good color for the relationship, knowledge, helpful people and children areas. Yellow symbolizes wisdom and is a stimulating color that inspires mental clarity and energy. Yellow gathers people together and also represents patience.

Solid objects

Heavy, solid objects are an invaluable feng shui cure when you are feeling insecure. They will bring stability when placed in any area where there is too much movement. Objects like statues and carvings may be stone, concrete, wood, ceramic or metal (depending on the element of the area in which they are being placed).

Heavy, solid objects make you feel more "grounded," so they are particularly helpful if you live at the top of a tall building or if the room beneath your bedroom is unoccupied. They are also very useful in bringing some stability into your life when you are starting a new job, or are feeling insecure about your employment, or if your relationships are going through a tricky phase. For example, to ensure a solid marriage place a pair of rocks or statues in the relationship area if it is the woman who is not so "solid" or may be wandering. Put them in the helpful people area if it is the man who needs to be "grounded." When you place a heavy object somewhere, consider the color and subject as well. Think about whether it is appropriate for that area in your home.

A bead curtain hung in a doorway or across a corridor between two doors effectively slows down the movement of chi.

Revolving and moving objects

This category of feng shui cures covers a multitude of objects including mobiles, fountains, toy windmills, electric fans, bead curtains and even lengths of dangling ribbon. Their shared attribute is that they can all circulate, redirect or (in the case of bead curtains) slow down chi in one way or another. This means that they are extremely effective cures in any home that has stagnant areas or too much movement. Most revolving and moving objects provide a double cure, because they make sounds which have their own value in circulating or altering the direction of energy in the rooms in your home.

Windmills placed near your front door outside in the garden, or even in a window box, will stimulate chi towards the house bringing opportunity and people to your door. Likewise, a fountain near your front door will encourage chi inwards, provided that the water is flowing towards the house. Windmills do not have to be ornate, expensive garden ornaments—the toys that children play with are just as effective.

Symbols

Whatever we put around us we tend to recreate so we need to be very sensitive to the artwork in our homes. Pictures need to be pertinent to what we want to create in that room. For example, it is not appropriate to fill our offices with photos of sexy men or women as they will distract us from our work. In the same way, it would not be good to have a gloomy painting of someone crying in our sitting room. A better choice would perhaps be of a family playing cards together, a group of friends happily dancing or simply cheering scenes of beautiful countryside, animals or birds.

Think about the walls in your home and what these symbols are saying to you and your visitors. Bare walls are more likely to make you feel lonely or depressed, but the wrong picture in the wrong room can also create a negative atmosphere. The composition, coloring and elements in a picture can all have a strong influence on the energy in your home. This doesn't just apply to silk embroideries, paintings, photographs or anything you might hang on a wall. Statues and ornaments of animals, birds and gods bring their own energy to a room and where you position them is very important. In Part Two, you will find feng shui cures that involve hanging particular images or placing statues and carvings.

Good feng shui practice

- Be bold and give or throw away pictures or symbols that are not benefiting you.
- Keep the glass and frames of paintings clean and don't forget to remove dust from silk hangings and ornaments.
- If a painting's protective glass is damaged, replace it.

The dragon and the phoenix are two of the four "spiritually endowed" creatures. The others are the unicorn and the tortoise (or turtle).

Cleansing

Buildings, just like our cars, clothes and dirty dishes, need to be cleansed from time to time to rid them of negative vibrations and stagnant energy that inevitably accumulate and influence us. The ritual of cleaning is an important aspect of feng shui and also forms part of other cultures like those of the Native Americans. There are simple and more complicated cleansing procedures, depending on how much time and effort you are prepared to put into the cleansing. If you feel you cannot cope, you could always ask a professional to come and cleanse your home for you.

Incense is a powerful feng shui cure and plays a vital role in the cleansing ritual.

A simple cleansing procedure

Incense cleanses invisible vibrations and is an integral part of a thorough cleaning. It works on a deep level and only needs to be burnt occasionally. It is considered a fragrant messenger to the gods and should always be burnt with a mental request for help and guidance towards any act. So when you are cleansing a house or room, you need to request assistance in the cleansing.

Here are basic instructions on how to cleanse your home (if you prefer, you can concentrate on just one room at a time). You will need three purifying incense sticks about 12 inches long; a white candle; three flowers (a red one for life and happiness, a yellow one for joy and laughter and a white one for cleansing and healing); a mayan ball (see pages 126 and 134 where this is described); some bells; and extra incense or a smudge stick (see opposite).

1   Clean the house from top to bottom and open the windows to allow the chi (energy) to move freely.

2   Wash your hands, arms and face (if possible, take a shower so that you are clean all over). Take off any jewelry and your shoes, as these will have absorbed their own negative energy.

3   Protect yourself during the cleansing process by wearing a mayan ball.

4 Burn one stick of purifying incense and a white candle in the center of each floor of the house, or at the front door, back door and center of your apartment, if you live on one level. Or you can put one at the front and back of the apartment and the third by an open window.

As you light them, dedicate the incense and candle to the house spirits, your ancestors and guides. All homes have something which you might call atmosphere or house spirits. You can judge your reception by seeing if you feel warm in your heart as you make your dedication. If you feel tension, keep introducing yourself to the spirits until you feel warm and relaxed.

5 Place the flowers beside the candle to absorb negative vibrations. After the cleansing, wrap the flowers in tissue paper and throw them away.

6 Starting at the front door, burn a smudge stick or some incense and waft it along all the walls of the house. Keep repeating your intention to cleanse the house while you do this. When you get back to the front door, wave the incense in a figure-of-eight pattern.

7 Clean your face, arms and hands. Give thanks for any assistance in the cleansing.

8 Repeat Steps 6 and 7, first by chanting an invoking mantra like *Om manee padme hum* around the house. Now repeat the steps with loud hand claps to get the stagnant energy moving. In each part of the house, start with a low clap, then one a little higher and finally clap as high as you can. Repeat the steps again, this time using a large bell. Then repeat with a small bell. Remember to cleanse yourself after each cleansing stage.

9 After the cleansing, protect your home by hanging bagua mirrors (see pages 23 and 43). Finally, cleanse yourself by soaking in a salty bath for at least ten minutes and then rinsing off under a cool shower.

Times to cleanse

There are certain times when it is particularly important to cleanse your home and rid the atmosphere of negative vibrations. These include:
- when you first move into a house;
- when a relationship ends;
- after an illness (sometimes also during an illness);
- after an unpleasant visitor.

You should also cleanse your home:
- if the building stands on the site of a former burial ground (or anything that can be connected to death like a funeral parlor or butcher's shop) or if it used to be a prison or hospital;
- if there has been an early death or murder in the house;
- or if you just have a feeling of uneasiness or any negativity.

Using a smudge stick

Smudge sticks are thick bundles of herbs (usually sage and sweet grass) that are tied with cotton. To use a smudge stick:
- light the end so the flame burns brightly, then blow out the flame so the stick is just smoldering;
- at all times, hold a heatproof container under the end of the stick to catch falling ash;
- blow or waft the smoke in the desired direction;
- extinguish the stick safely after use.

Part Two: creative solutions

These quick feng shui cures are listed according to the bagua areas. So before you can put any of the cures into practice, you need to establish which areas of your home relate to the areas of the bagua by drawing a plan of your house or apartment and laying the bagua template over it (see pages 16–17). The introduction to each area also explains what it means if the area is missing or has extended areas. Each cure is accompanied by a brief description of what each cure is best used for.

In this section of the book, you will also find out how to access your best directions and use feng shui to advantage at key events in our lives—New Year's, weddings, funerals, Christmas and christenings. There are also tips on how to make dinner parties successful, the best presents to give people (according to their Chinese sign of the zodiac), how to apply feng shui to your handbag or car, and the feng shui interpretations of fashion statements.

Developing your career

Career area

This area relates to your vocation and your life path and all the things that you do during your daily duties. This may be working at a job from nine until five; it may be being a full-time parent or perhaps studying all day as a student. The career area is sometimes called the journey because it also relates to everything that you have learned and experienced so far in life—including love, study and illness—that has brought you to where you are today. The career area also relates to the health of our bones, kidneys, hearing, will power and constitution.

The career area is at the center front part of your home (see pages 16–17). It also encompasses the area around your front door and your telephone, fax and computer, which are all "front doors" that people access. Ninety percent of the energy in your building comes in through these "doors." You walk energy into your home; friends bring laughter; illness can come in; you enter and leave with money in your pocket; your mail is delivered. Even if your front door falls in the helpful people or knowledge area, it will still influence your career, though it will be colored by the area in which it is actually sited.

To examine this area you need to ask yourself some questions. First, are you happy in your job? If you really look forward to your daily tasks for five working days out of seven, then you have a good energy in this area. If you don't, perhaps it is because things are happening too quickly and you feel under pressure to get all your duties completed. Or maybe everything is too quiet and you are are bored. Or your job may not be safe—you might be under the threat of redundancy or dismissal. If any of these cases are pertinent to you, then cures need to be applied in your career area. Similarly, if you have some weakness in the health aspects listed above, you also need to examine this area of your home.

Missing   Extended

An outdoor fountain with water pouring from a lion's mouth.

If the area is missing, the people living here will find it more difficult to find a totally satisfying job. Their general health will be weaker because the area affects the kidneys (which contain our life essence) and governs our constitution. Our hearing and bones may become weaker and we can become less virile. It is usually more difficult to find your life path. And finances can be a problem.

If the area is extended, the residents will tend to enjoy strong health. They will be able to acquire a reasonable amount of money, and on top of that they will tend to spend it wisely. They will be open to spiritual things and have clear views and goals.

Quick cures

A crystal chandelier is a useful cure if your job and life are generally too quiet and few opportunities seem to be coming your way. Hang a chandelier with one, three, five, six or seven bulbs near the entrance to your home. Crystals create movement and strengthen intuition while light always draws more energy to an area. One and three are numbers of growth and six and seven are metal numbers that feed the career area energetically.
Best used for bringing inspirational opportunity into your life.

Wind chimes will help if there is a lot of stress in your life and you are too quiet or too busy. If it is placed carefully, it will help to create controlled movement within your career and general life. If you choose a metal chime, make sure that the tubes are hollow so that they can transcendentally raise the chi and encourage you up the ladder. But take care not to use large wind chimes because they can damage your liver and create quarrels. Hang the wind chimes just inside the front door in such a way that the clapper lightly touches the top and makes the chimes tinkle softly each time the door opens and closes.
Best used for bringing in controlled opportunity to your life and to protect health.

A fountain placed near the front door should help if life seems a bit of a struggle and nothing is flowing. It will generally bring more opportunity and satisfaction to every aspect of your life. If the fountain has a spout, make sure that the water is pouring into the house rather than out of the front door. Water influences money so water energetically pouring out of the house means money will flow out of your house and so is not positive feng shui.

Wind chimes hung above a door so the clapper will just be touched when the door opens and closes.

This dragon-headed turtle has blue ribbon in his mouth to bring good health to the people in the house.

Some time ago I visited a small stockbrokerage firm that was experiencing considerable problems. Among the things I asked them to do was to place a round fountain at a particular point in their foyer. The changes were made and business picked up in a way the CEO had not seen since the company moved there five years earlier. He firmly believes that feng shui saved the business.

Best used for strengthening health, career and finances.

A mirror hung opposite the front door will bring in more opportunities. This mirror should be large and framed, preferably in gold or silver. Generally, its height should be geater than its width. Mirrors always reflect everything opposite them very effectively. You may even have seen young children and animals run into mirrors because they are so fooled by the reflection that they really believe that there is another room in the mirror. Mirrors create a virtual reality; they expand an area and draw energy towards them. This will result in more opportunity coming into your home energetically.

Best used for bringing more opportunity relating to career, relationships and everything.

A dragon-headed turtle placed inside the front door, perhaps on a console table or a bookshelf, will bring in more options. The dragon symbolizes luck, the turtle long life and the baby turtle new beginnings. In the daytime, the dragon-headed turtle should face the front door. If you want luck, place a piece of gold ribbon in his mouth; for happy relationships use a piece of red ribbon and use blue ribbon for improved health. In the evening, turn him around to face the interior. Avoid placing him in front of a bathroom or kitchen door. According to legend, if you respect the dragon-headed turtle, he will bestow blessings upon you.

Best used for new beginnings and luck.

Up-lights are among the most useful cures for those who live in a basement apartment. If this is you, it could be one of the reasons your career and life is quiet. Having to step down from street level into your home can create stagnation, so it needs constant attention to prevent it from becoming damp and stale. This type of energy is not good for relationships, career or health so you should install up-lights outside the front door on both sides. Make sure the house number is as high as possible. You could put it just above the front door or even above a window that is parallel to the street so it is visible to passersby. Each time they read the number, they help to raise the apartment energetically. Another cure for basements is to create an artificial step just outside the threshold so you have to step up and over it to walk into the apartment.

Best used for strengthening health, relationships and career.

Two heavy stone objects will help make your job more secure during times of recession. Ideally, place these objects (deer, dogs, cranes, dragons and turtles are good) on either side of your front door. Alternatively, put one heavy item just inside the front door but not so that it will create an obstruction. You could simply put a bust or a statue on a sideboard. The objects must be of sufficient weight that you need to use two hands to lift each. One of my clients used this cure when major redundancies were being made at her company and she was one of the 25 percent that were kept on.

Best used for stability during recession.

An empty bowl or vase will bring new beginnings into your life. Place one or two bowls, preferably made from pottery, outside your front door. This is a specially good cure if your house faces southwest, west, northwest or northeast.

Best used for totally new beginnings.

Place an empty, heavy stone jar on both sides of your front door.

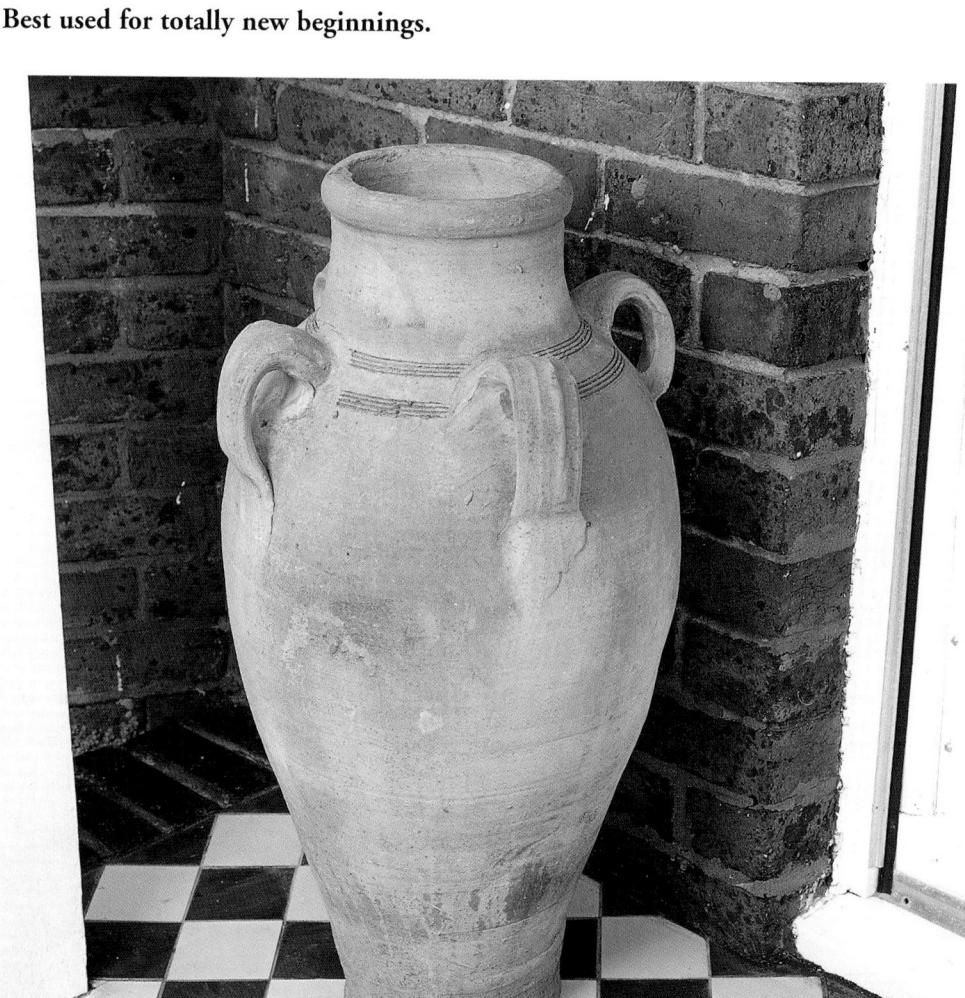

A solid front door can make a huge difference to your life. If you generally feel insecure and that events are beyond your control, you might simply need to replace your front door. If it is mainly glass, it will be creating instability. Things like romance and money will tend to come in to your life and go straight out again, and your health may be delicate. Chi behaves like light in many respects and it can pass through glass very easily. A solid front door will make everything much stronger and more stable.

From a mundane perspective it is undesirable for your visitors to catch sight of you before you see them, especially if they are unwelcome. Also, if callers can look into your home, they are entering your home energetically. Have you ever felt irritated when someone has stared at your car, or any of your belongings, for longer than feels comfortable? This is because that stare carries the person's energy to the object of attention. You may not want such an intrusion in your home.

A solid front door makes you more stable and protected than one with glass panels.

Best used for stability, security and protection.

A bagua mirror is one of the simplest and most powerful feng shui cures. Examine the area around your home and see if there are any sharp corners pointing at it. This might be from a neighbor's roof or the corner of a building. If this is the case, hang a bagua mirror just above your front door or in the window nearest to the potentially detrimental element to deflect the negative energy away. Electric poles, roads, railroad stations, police stations, hospitals and prisons also generate negative energy that can be warded off by hanging a bagua mirror. Outdoor bagua mirrors usually have plastic frames (which survive for longer than wooden ones). Balance and harmony are all important in feng shui, so if the mirror is going to be an eyesore or not in keeping with your home, it is quite acceptable to place it behind a creeper or foliage on an outside wall.

A bagua mirror deflects negative energy and protects your home.

Best used for protecting the whole family.

A boat charm helps you to overcome obstacles in life.

A boat charm, which includes a sailing boat laden with wonderful merchandise in barrels and boxes, symbolizes plain sailing. In the same way that the boat parts the waves, it cuts through obstacles in your career and personal relationships. It represents a safe and rewarding journey through life and this is reinforced by the name of the charm. Hang it in the hall.

Best used for creating safe and satisfying career opportunities.

Two mayan balls are a useful cure if you have windows on either side of your front door. Such windows can create instability and vulnerability, and the feng shui is especially negative if the windows reach all the way down to the floor. Hang one ball on red ribbon or thread in each window.

Best used for protection.

Two evergreen plants placed on either side of, or just inside, your front door are good feng shui if life is moving too fast. Water is the element that the career area belongs to, so the plants will absorb excessive energy, create more balance and alleviate stress. The largest plant (one is always slightly bigger than the other) should go on the right side of the door as you face the house. Choose fairly large plants that are at least a third of the height of the door.

Best used for slowing life down to a healthy pace.

Wind chimes and a bagua mirror will help if you often enter your home via the garage as well as the front door. Entering from the garage can create negative energy caused by fumes from the car and this negativity can taint the energy in the house. Entering through this door can also create confusion regarding which life path you should be taking. It is always best to enter through the front door. If this is not feasible, make sure there is an extractor fan in the garage (or at least plenty of good ventilation) and that the area you walk into from the garage is spacious. Place the mirror above the door to the house so it is shining towards the garage entrance. Hang the wind chimes so that the clapper touches the top of the door.

Best used for strengthening the health and intuition of occupants and helping you out of a dead-end job.

A decluttering session is essential if the first room you walk into as you enter the house is a laundry, utility room or anywhere generally messy. This is because the clutter has the influence of "flattening" and depressing the chi which can have a corresponding effect on your life. Remove all the clutter or at the very least conceal it in cupboards.

Best used for alleviating depression associated with work and life generally.

A weather vane in an appropriate shape will bring more career opportunities, give you more self-esteem, make you stronger and enable you to receive more support. The following groupings of animals form what are known as the four tri-harmonies. Find out what animal you are (see pages 88–91) and use a weather vane that includes this. The tri-harmonies are: 1. Dragon, monkey and rat; 2. Ox, snake and rooster; 3. Rabbit, goat/sheep and pig; 4. Tiger, horse and dog. Site the weather vane high up and as close as possible to your front door. If you are faced with a choice of animals, choose the one that supports the breadwinner in the household.

Best used for giving you more clarity over your career choice, making you aim high and giving you protection.

A rooster weather vane is best for those who are an ox, snake or rooster according to the Chinese zodiac.

年年有餘

歲歲吉祥年年歡　年年有餘歲歲長

Hanging a picture of nine lucky fish is a good alternative to having a fish tank.

A picture of nine fish is a very positive image to place near the entrance to your home. Three times three! Three is the most potent male yang number. It represents growth and movement, and also some jealousy, aggression and tension (all of which are often necessary in business). The number nine signifies the culmination or the highest pinnacle. Ideally, one of the nine fish should be black to protect your health and career, and to ensure that the wealth aspect does not become too dominant. The color of the black fish also distinguishes it from the eight other fish. Eight is the most auspicious number—it signifies eternal wealth both physically and spiritually.

Best used for bringing more activity into your life and increasing your earnings.

Christmas lights are not just for the Christmas tree! Many people have consulted me in some agitation when they have heard that having a tree opposite their front door can block their career. In fact, this all depends on the tree. If the tree radiates beauty it is fine; if it radiates gloom then it is not. You don't have to cut down the tree to neutralize this influence. You could simply prune it so sunshine can stream through or hang crystals from the branches. You could also entwine Christmas lights among the branches or install outdoor spotlights that are positioned to shine upwards through the tree.

Best used for when your life is unsatisfying and everything seems hard work.

An elephant derives most of his strength from his trunk. He is a symbol of strength, sagacity and prudence and is one of the four animals representing power and energy. Legend says that the elephant is the bearer of the wish-granting gem and that if you put whatever you want on the back of an elephant your wish will come true. So you might place on your elephant a healthy evergreen plant for good health, a coin for more money, a stone for an easy pregnancy, or a crystal to improve your career. Always keep the elephant near a window or your front door.

Best used for strengthening your career by making you stronger and more grounded.

A clear glass paperweight placed in the hall will strengthen your intuition and help you to make good decisions.
Best used for when you have a boring job and life.

A white vase with blue flowers will strengthen any kidney and arthritic conditions, if placed quite near the front door. You can use either fresh or artificial flowers but remember that the latter only last for about six months (after which cleanse or replace them).
Best used for strengthening kidney and bone weaknesses.

Paintings and posters of boats can have a very good effect on your career. Water energizes the career area and a boat in full sail indicates a happy, healthy and fascinating journey through life. The boat needs to be loaded with goodies (a cargo of barrels or boxes) signifying success in life. The boat must be sailing towards you rather than away, so don't position the picture so that the boat is on course to sail out of your front door!
Best used for encouraging employment that is rewarding, satisfying and always moving on.

Check that a glass paperweight won't roll on to the floor. Put it on a mirror to increase its energy.

If you can't find a picture or poster of a sailing boat, a wooden carving of a boat works just as well.

Accessing your best directions

According to the Ghanzi Compass School of Feng Shui, there are eight directions that have signficance. Four are beneficial (good directions) and four are harmful (bad directions). Identifying and implementing your positive directions and avoiding the harmful ones can generate good fortune.

People are basically divided into two groups: East and West. Within these two groups are sub-categories of nine additional groups. These are calculated according to your date of birth. There is a unique vibration emanating from the compass directions that will influence us in a positive or negative way.

Your good directions

The best direction is called your *sheng chi* (generating breath). It is known as your millionaire's direction and it means success in everything—money, love and family relationships but especially money and self-empowerment. It is also an area you should use within your home for your office or bedroom.

The second direction is *tien yi* (doctor from heaven). It means good health of mind and body. This is the direction you would access if you were suffering from a prolonged or inexplicable illness. It is good to have the back of your stove (where the power supply comes in) facing this direction.

The third direction is known as *nien yen* (longevity with rich descendants). This direction brings good relationships, romantic and otherwise, and increases the chances of having children.

The fourth direction is called *fu wei* (star of wisdom). It brings personal development and clarity. This can mean you will undergo some learning experiences. This direction is recommended for students or executives to bring them clarity of thought and to help them to assimilate facts.

Your bad directions

The first direction in the chart is *chueh ming* (total loss). It is the worst direction so avoid it if at all possible.

The second worst direction is *lui sha* (six killings). It can mean grievous harm to the family and family business.

The third worst direction is *wu kuei* (five ghosts). You may suffer from burglary, fire, or any general attack upon yourself and your property. There will probably be quarrels within the household and your employees will not be loyal.

The least bad direction is *ho hai* (accidents and mishaps). Even though you win you still lose. You may win a court case but you will still lose money or reputation.

Use one of your good directions if you possibly can. For example, if you were born in 1963, your *sheng chi* is southeast, so first of all try to live in a house that faces this direction. Next position your bed so that when you lie down your toes are pointing northwest and your head is to the southeast. To activate good luck at work, position your desk so you are looking to the southeast.

In the chart opposite, you will find your year of birth. The western calendar does not coincide with the Chinese, so if you were born between 1 January and about 4 February (the Chinese New Year), look in the year before. For example, if you were born in January 1960 you should look at the directions for 1959.

Special note

Do not use the south in 1999, the north in 2000, the southwest in 2001, the east in 2002, the southeast in 2003, the northwest in 2005, the west in 2006 or the northeast in 2007 even if it represents your best direction, otherwise it may bring some bad luck. All directions are fine in 2004.

If you are a man   ## If you are a woman

If you were born in:	Your best directions are:				Your worst directions are:				Your best directions are:				Your worst directions are:			
	Sheng chi	Tien yi	Nien yen	Fu wei	Chueh ming	Lui sha	Wu kuei	Ho hai	Sheng chi	Tien yi	Nien yen	Fu wei	Chueh ming	Lui sha	Wu kuei	Ho hai
1900, 1909, 1918, 1927, 1936, 1945, 1954, 1963, 1972, 1981, 1990, 1999	SE	E	S	N	W	NE	NW	SW	SW	NW	W	NE	SE	E	N	S
1901, 1910, 1919, 1928, 1937, 1946, 1955, 1964, 1973, 1982, 1991, 2000	E	SE	N	S	NE	W	SW	NW	W	NE	SW	NW	S	N	E	SE
1902, 1911, 1920, 1929, 1938, 1947, 1956, 1965, 1974, 1983, 1992, 1991, 2001	SW	NW	W	NE	SE	E	N	S	NW	SW	NE	W	E	SE	S	N
1903, 1912, 1921, 1930, 1939, 1948, 1957, 1966, 1975, 1984, 1993, 2002	NW	SW	NE	W	E	SE	S	N	SW	NW	W	NE	SE	E	N	S
1904, 1913, 1922, 1931, 1940, 1949, 1958, 1967, 1976, 1985, 1994, 2003	W	NE	SW	NW	S	N	E	SE	E	SE	N	S	NE	W	SW	NW
1905, 1914, 1923, 1932, 1941, 1950, 1959, 1968, 1977, 1986, 1995, 2004	NE	W	NW	SW	N	S	SE	E	SE	E	S	N	W	NE	NW	W
1906, 1915, 1924, 1933, 1942, 1951, 1960, 1969, 1978, 1987, 1996, 2005	N	S	E	SE	NE	W	SW	NW	NE	W	NW	SW	N	S	SE	E
1907, 1916, 1925, 1934, 1943, 1952, 1961, 1970, 1979, 1988, 1997, 2006	S	N	SE	E	W	NE	NW	SW	S	N	SE	E	W	NE	NW	SW
1908, 1917, 1926, 1935, 1944, 1953, 1962, 1971, 1980, 1989, 1998, 2007	NE	W	NW	SW	N	S	SE	E	N	S	E	SE	NE	W	SW	NW

Encouraging productivity

Beautiful things inspire us, so make sure there is something wonderful to look at in the office. You will feel happier, look forward to being at your desk and therefore be in a better frame of mind to work most effectively.

Cures for the home office

If your office is not in a different building but in part of your home, it is like a microcosm within the macrocosm of your house. Although it is part of your home, it is essentially separate. Wherever it falls within your home, it will be influencing that facet of your life.

As it is a complete environment, it needs to be treated as an entity of its own. This means you need to place the bagua over the entrance of the room as though it were the front door to identify the relevant areas. Your office should be regarded as a chairman's office. Nothing should be dumped in here and it should be treated with respect. It is where you generate your income and you may spend eight or more hours a day here so it needs to be a clear, vibrant place.

Chrysanthemums in the fame area of the office will bring riches and laughter. If they are bought or picked on October 9 and kept in a vase for 27 days, they are said to bring a position of high rank. As the flowers start to wilt, replace them with fresh blooms. **Best used for gaining a promotion.**

Place your Chinese zodiac animal on your desk (see pages 88–91 to find out what you are). This is a crystal dragon.

A picture of a mountain behind your desk will make you stronger. As you approach your desk you will see this picture which subconsciously makes you think you are unmovable and will be in the director's seat for a long time. It has the added advantage of also making those people who approach your desk subconsciously feel that you have the strength and endurance of a mountain.
Best used for strengthening your position and gaining more respect.

The Chinese zodiac animal that correlates to your year of birth will give you a stronger sense of self and more power. The animal should be glass or crystal and sit on an octagonal mirror. Place this on a piece of red cloth or paper on the far right-hand corner of your desk.
Best used for giving you a stronger sense of self, more staying power and strengthening your intuition.

When you place turtle guardians on a display mirror, always arrange them so they are facing inwards, and are looking towards each other.

Turtle guardians are potent symbols of longevity and learned wisdom. Each one represents a different phase in our lives, from youthful impetuosity to feelings of solemnity and wisdom. They remind us that we will consistently oscillate between these different phases and support us through each cycle. You can either place turtle guardians in the career area of your home, or home office, or display them behind your desk. They will generally help to strengthen your position in life. It is said that the turtle's shell represents the vault of the universe (the sky or heavens) and its body the earth; it moves through water (the sea) and according to Chinese legend, it lives for 10,000 years.

Best used for reminding you to pace yourself and to "move" in harmony with the cycles of nature by realizing that there are times to expand and times to rest.

A carp painting does not have to be a traditional picture. Hanging a decorated plate on a wall is also an effective cure.

A carp painting symbolizes perseverence and money (or gain). On its journey upstream the carp has to jump the rapids and, according to legend, when it completes this maneuver it turns into a celestial dragon. This feat can be compared to success in business or examinations. A picture of a carp surrounded by shoals of smaller fish (those who do not succeed) is particularly helpful. Ideally the picture should be hung opposite your desk and should depict three or nine fish. If there are nine, there should be one black fish and the remaining eight should be orange or gold.

Best used for passing exams or taking your company to new heights.

A chandelier combining faceted crystals or glass with light brightens, lifts and strengthens the energy. It encourages you to look up and is specially good when rooms need to be healed. An holistic clinic that I visited in 1996 was having problems with very difficult clients. The practitioners were depressed and as a consequence they were not able to do their jobs efficiently. Among the cures that were applied, we hung the most breathtakingly stunning chandelier. Almost immediately, the attitude of the patients changed and this had a correspondingly positive effect on the practitioners. **Best used for combating depression.**

A carp pot in which to store pens is a valuable quick cure. Simply place it by the telephone at home or on your desk in the office. According to feng shui, fish can be compared to the king's subjects and the art of angling can be likened to the art of ruling. Thus an unskilled angler will catch no fish and a tactless employer or king will fail to win

Tips for your office

- To keep in a position of power and control, sit in the emperor position. This means sitting as far as possible into the room so that you have a good view of the door and window from your position at your desk.
- To discreetly increase your chances of gaining a promotion, raise the level of your desk and chair by a few inches. Bring some chocks of wood to work and slip one under each leg of your desk. Adjust the height of your chair to compensate.
- If you want to get people to follow your lead and show more respect towards you, do not sit with your back to the door. If you cannot move your desk then hang a mirror so that you can see what is going on behind you.
- Place an illuminated globe that shows the countries of the world in the fame area of your office or home. This will encourage bigger markets for special projects and bring opportunities for your career and future. It is preferable to use a globe that rotates.

over his people. The carp is a symbol of two martial attributes, perseverance and success, because of its ability to swim upstream and win. Once the fish succeeds in passing above the rapids it is transformed into a "dragon" of great distinction and eminence.

A very powerful and difficult man invited me to consult in his huge offices in the city because he was having problems keeping his staff. In his view, almost all of them were inefficient, insubordinate and stupid. First, I told him about the Chinese art of war, which is never to disagree obviously by saying, "You are wrong," or "That's not true," but only to say tactful things like, "Mmm that's interesting," or "Yes, I agree, and have you thought of…?" Then, among the other suggestions I recommended, he bought a carp pen pot and a dragon pen holder to remind him of this basic strategy. He has them to this day, and though he is still impatient, he is much more compassionate and understanding. Most importantly, he has been able to win the admiration and loyalty of most of his staff.

Best used for becoming a good leader or employer.

A carp pot (left) and dragon and cloud pen holder (right) will make you a better employer and help to keep you organized.

A dragon and cloud pen holder will improve your office environment. The celestial dragon is a creature unseen in this world. From its vantage point in the heavens it sees all four corners of the earth. It is endowed with extraordinary powers of strength, courage and wisdom. It is the spirit of change and it guides us through important decisions. The emperors of long ago would decorate their palaces with dragons to attract great good fortune. The dragon must always be seen with a representation of the invaluable pearl which has exuded from its mouth. The pearl was distilled from the essence of the moon and on the holder is represented by the place where you would traditionally keep ink, but today might prefer to keep paperclips.

Best used for if you are a poor decision maker.

Three lucky gold coins (right) will benefit your finances. The extraordinary walnut (far right) will help when you need to keep your wits about you.

Three gold coins linked with red ribbon should be placed on the left-hand corner of your desk on an octagonal or round display mirror and/or fixed to your "money in" book. I always keep a set in my change purse as well. If your business has a cash till, you could also place three coins in the far left corner.

Best used for increasing finances.

The extraordinary walnut has engraved upon it 100 of the cleverest men who will combine all their wisdom to support and help you. Keep one in your pocket when you need to be extra sharp, maybe during a court case, exam, driving test or an important business meeting.

Best used for giving you the advantage.

A spherical faceted crystal hung in the window will bring in more movement and activity. Crystals are often undervalued, but they have an extraordinary power especially considering they are so small. They stop you from being too single-minded, they open up opportunities and raise the level of energy in the environment. A Swiss business man I visited tripled his business in a few months after using a significant amount of faceted crystals in the wealth area of the office. It was quite a sight to see—at certain times of the day it was a vision of colors and light. He also put lots of big plants near the very busy photocopier in this area.

Best used for raising the chi and creating a healthier and more active environment.

Deciding on a job

Walking between potential workplace buildings will help you if you are trying to decide between two jobs that you have been offered. Walk around each building and see how you feel. You will notice that one building seems more comfortable so you will generally feel more in tune with one than the other.

One or two small bells hung on your office door will encourage good fortune to enter. Tie them on to the outside doorknob with red ribbon. Symbolically the sound of the bell heralds prosperity and good news. Don't use large bells. And if your good directions are east or southeast and your office door also faces one of these, use wooden or pottery bells or wooden windchimes.

Best used for inviting good fortune.

Hang small bells from your office doorkknob or handle to encourage good luck.

A large evergreen plant should feature in every office—and more than one if you have the space. Palms are particularly good because they tend to spread more at the top. A plant that reaches waist height spreads the energy at waist height whereas a plant that nearly reaches the ceiling spreads the energy at head height—a much better place to have energy in an office. If the plant is not sufficiently tall, stand it on a pedestal to gain the extra height.

Best used for improving health and making you think bigger thoughts.

A lava lamp in your home office will encourage different things depending on where it is sited. Place it in the fame area if you need publicity or promotion, in the relationship area if you need to do more networking, or in the wealth area if you need growth.

Best used for creating activity in an area of your choice.

A candle will help to keep you at work when you would much prefer to stop.

A candle burning on your desk will have a gathering effect when you need to stay at your desk for a long time. It will encourage you to work until the task in hand is completed.

Best used for making you finish your work.

A fish tank containing three goldfish and two dark fish is a useful addition to the home office. The goldfish are to encourage money and the dark fish balance them (so that any wealth does not become too dominant). The dark fish also protect relationships and help to keep your constitution strong. Place the tank in the area that is to your far left as you are sitting at your desk. The fish should be healthy and happy for your finances to flourish. If they outgrow the tank, give them to someone who has room for them and then replace the fish.

Best used for increasing finances.

New Year's

According to the complex Chinese calendar, the new year begins on the first day of the second new moon after the winter solstice (December 22)—and not on January 1. Try these suggestions if you would like to optimize your luck for the new year.

- For 15 days before New Year's Day (which is usually between January 24 and February 15), Chinese people cleanse their houses. This involves extensive cleaning. There is a floor sweeping day, a window cleaning day, a furniture cleaning day, a repairing day and eventually a flower placing day. You don't have to spend the whole of every day cleaning, but it does need to be done thoroughly.

- Debts are best paid off (it used to be customary for employees to receive a bonus towards this end). And all arguments and worries should be resolved lest they influence the good luck of the coming year.

- On New Year's Day, everyone should rest. No housework should be done in case all the good luck is brushed, vacuumed or washed away.

- Cooking is put to one side (food has to be prepared the day before). No scissors or knives can be used (they have a potentially threatening nature, which can contribute to tension and stress). Everyone takes care not to fall out or quarrel and is careful not to break or tear anything. This is because it is believed that whatever occurs on this day will somehow set a precedent for the rest of the year.

Clean your home thoroughly for the 15 days before Chinese New Year's.

- Traditionally, a grand feast including carp or salmon (for longevity and intelligence), cabbage (for fortune and riches) and oranges or mandarins (for good health) is eaten for good luck. Nutrition books agree that fish is good food for the brain, cabbage for the stomach and liver and oranges are filled with vitamin C—a vitamin that builds the immune system.

- No meat is eaten on New Year's Day as a sign of respect for animals.

- Wishes and resolutions are always made for the new year. They are carefully written on a piece of paper that is then placed in a red envelope (it has to be red to bring the resolutions to life) and burnt. When you go through the five steps of this process you are energetically completing and empowering the resolutions.
  STEP 1 Find pieces of paper, a pen and red envelopes.
  STEP 2 Think carefully.
  STEP 3 Write down each resolution.
  STEP 4 Put each resolution into a red envelope.
  STEP 5 Burn the envelopes. This seals each resolution, makes it permanent and means you will complete the action.

Here are a few suggestions for New Year's resolutions that incorporate good feng shui:

1 Get rid of your clutter (or at least try to get each room down to only 10 percent clutter).

2 Lead by example for the whole year. (It does not help your children, family or colleagues if you say one thing and behave in another way. If you really want to change or influence someone, the best way to do it is to show them by your example.)

3 Have some fun every week—perhaps by playing golf or dancing. Do something purely for your pleasure and just for fun—not to get fit or to further your education.

4 Be kind to your parents and grandparents. They love you more than anyone in the world.

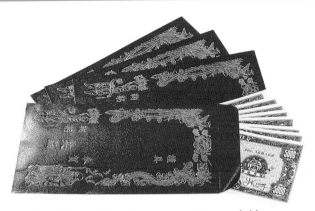

Red envelopes with lucky money are given to children until they are married to bring them luck.

5 Make one resolution a seemingly impossible dream—like getting married within the year even if you don't have a partner at the moment, or running your own profitable business even though you are unemployed right now.

6 Exchange your love, money and knowledge in abundance. There are four levels of exchange that can be related to all aspects of life:

- The first level is serious under-exchange; you go into an art gallery and steal a painting. Or you pretend to be madly in love with someone just to further your own ends.

- The second level is under-exchange; when you know the painting is worth $1,000 but you bargain until you get the price down to $500.

- The third level is fair exchange; the painting is worth $1,000 and you pay $1,000.

- The fourth level is exchanging in abundance; the painting is worth $1,000 but you love and appreciate it so much that you pay $1,200 for it. The emotional equivalent of this example is when someone close to you lets you down and you still give love to them.

7 Make sure you have some fortune cookies to serve at supper so that you can find out what the year has in store for you and to stimulate conversation.

8 If you successfully manage to force a narcissus to bloom so that it coincides with the new year, it is believed to indicate good fortune for the following 12 months.

9 Fire crackers are let off to "spring clean" the year. So why not have a firework display in the garden on New Year's Eve? With the smoke (incense), the bright lights, colors (fire) and the noise, you have nearly all the ingredients needed for cleansing.

10 On the second day of the new year, the Chinese go around visiting, gambling and generally having fun to set a precedent for the year. This is to encourage risk taking. The Chinese have a greeting they often call out which is "May you live in interesting times"—and to do this you need to take some risks.

11 The third day of the new year is assigned to having your fortune told. The year is thought to have properly begun and the energy to have settled by this date so the fortune-teller can predict the future more accurately.

12 On the fourth day, a wonderful meal is usually cooked, and the kitchen acknowledged. The Chinese believe that there are house spirits in every home (in the West, we simply call them atmosphere). The most influential spirit is thought to live in the kitchen so the Chinese often "talk" to their kitchens; they say good morning, ask if it is happy and see if they get a warm feeling in their heart. The meal is cooked in a very relaxed, considered way.

13 On the fifth day, parents are visited and are taken gifts; a red-flowering plant for health, I Ching coins for wealth, and a dragon-headed turtle for happiness. This corresponds with the western tradition of taking coal, an orange and a coin to someone's house on New Year's Day.

14 In China, New Year's Day is everyone's birthday and the Chinese people customarily calculate their ages not from their actual birthday but from New Year's Day of the year in which they were born.

Mandarin oranges represent immortality and good fortune. So it is always best to accept one, even if you don't want to eat it immediately.

Improving your relationships

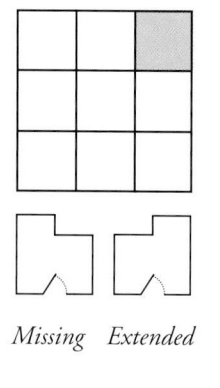

Missing   Extended

Relationship area

The relationship area of your home lies in the furthest right-hand corner from the front door (see also pages 16–17). This area relates to all one-to-one relationships, including those with a spouse, partner, employer, employee or best friend. It is the most feminine part of the house and needs to be warm and welcoming with lots of cushions and softness. The relationship area is associated with the earth element—specifically, black fertile earth that anything can grow in. The atmosphere here should be warm, still, safe and sumptuous.

If this area is missing, it can be difficult to find and hold on to a life partner. All one-to-one relationships can have a tendency to dissolve away and the stomach will gradually become weaker. It is usually difficult for a woman to be totally happy in this house unless cures are placed.

If this area is extended, then it can create problems. If a man and a woman live here, the woman's energy may become too strong and she will become too dominant, thus weakening the man and herself. An extended area will weaken the health of both sexes by creating overactivity in the stomach, and it may give one of them too big an appetite.

Months in which women should marry

RAT: July

OX: June

TIGER: February

RABBIT: March

DRAGON: May

SNAKE: October

HORSE: January

GOAT: December

MONKEY: September

ROOSTER: August

DOG: November

PIG: April

The ancient Chinese view of marriage

In all marriages in ancient China and many other countries in the world, *mei-jen* or matchmakers used to play a prominent role. First of all, astrological charts of the marriageable person would be carefully drawn up and complementary and harmonious matches were established. When this operation was completed and the couple were matched, the date of the wedding would be set. A lucky (yellow) day would be selected and an unlucky (black) day would be carefully avoided. This date would be sent on a yellow card to the parents of the groom and the bride.

Traditionally, depending on the year in which the bride was born, she would marry in a month that would bring her luck. In order to use this table you need to know which Chinese animal you are according to the Chinese calendar (see pages 88–91). Many still believe that if the wedding takes place in the month appropriate to the bride, it will be an auspicious start to the marriage.

Quick cures

A dragon-headed turtle will come to your rescue if your relationships are a bit

stagnant and you want them to develop or if you haven't got a partner at the moment. He can help you to accumulate long-lasting dynamic one-to-one relationships and new beginnings. The dragon symbolizes good luck and protection, the turtle represents long life and wisdom for relationships and a baby turtle brings all sorts of new beginnings. Put a dragon-headed turtle with a piece of red ribbon in his mouth in your bedroom or in the relationship area. He should look out of a window after dusk; in the morning turn him round so that he faces the interior or his energy will become exhausted. Respect the dragon-headed turtle and he can help make your dreams come true.

One of my clients is a beautiful, sensitive girl who had been stuck in a rut for about three years. She rarely went out and she was lonely. Among the changes I suggested was the placing of a dragon-headed turtle near her front door. In less than a month she had

Place a dragon-headed turtle facing out of a window at dusk and turn him to look inwards every morning.

taken up scuba diving, which she thoroughly enjoyed, and met a man (who also enjoyed scuba diving); she's now dating him on a regular basis.

Best used for bringing a new relationship in, or energizing an old one.

Cleansing your home is most important if a relationship has ended. You need to burn three incense sticks to remove negative energy and vibrations that have built up and are now causing stagnation in the atmosphere. Each stick has mantras and symbols embossed upon it requesting all kinds of good things. If you live in a house, burn incense on each floor; if you live in an apartment burn one in the front of your home and the others in the middle and at the back. As you burn the incense, ask your guides to assist you in overcoming the past relationship and give you the guidance you need. For further information on cleansing, see pages 34–35.

Best used for when a relationship is over and you are having difficulty moving on.

Bamboo growing in the relationship area of your garden (use the bagua to establish where this is) will bring elements of flexibility, durability, strength and grace to your relationships. Because bamboo is evergreen and flourishes during all seasons, it will bring enduring qualities too.

Best used for when there is jealousy or inflexibility in the relationship.

Bamboo in the relationship area of your garden will help to improve understanding between you and your partner.

A pair of stone rabbits (left) will help a relationship that seems to be falling apart, while a crystal mobile (right) is a useful cure to generate passion.

Stone or concrete objects have the ability to lend a grounding quality to an environment. Placing two heavy stone representations of friendly animals like rabbits in the relationship area will stop things from moving too fast when you want to create more stability, perhaps because a relationship is going through a change. Arrange the objects so that they are sitting close to each other. Suitable items include a boy and a girl (to represent a couple) or a pair of dolphins, swans, mandarin ducks, rabbits, dogs, phoenixes or doves. **Best used for a relationship that seems to be dissolving.**

Crystal mobiles can bring passion and sparkle into a relationship. Hang them from a length of silver thread in a sunny window of your bedroom or in a window in the relationship area of your home so that they can energize the room with prisms of sunlight. As the sun moves west the light will move round the room very slowly, thus preventing stagnation and energizing your relationships. Remember that crystals should always be faceted and spherical, like the crystal found in chandeliers. **Best used for bringing more sparkle and passion into your relationship.**

Replace your mattress or bed at the end of a relationship. While we are sleeping we "discharge" a lot of energy so the mattress will have become full of your partner's energy as well as your own. When a relationship ends, it is vital to make a fresh start. I visited a client who had been divorced almost ten years prior to my visit and she had still not gotten over her ex! I recommended many things but perhaps the most important was to get rid of the bed, which he had painstakingly made for her as a wedding gift. It was exquisite, extremely intricate, and even incorporated their names engraved within a heart. He had put a huge amount of love into it and my client had been sleeping in it since the marriage.

The bed had become very powerful with the energy of their love. So it was no wonder she had not managed to forget him. The bed just had to go. Less than six months after its departure she met someone she really liked at her bridge club. I don't know what has happened since, but the important thing is that she has finally been able to get over her ex-husband.

Best used for when you are starting a new relationship.

Red or pink flowers, preferably in a pink, white, glass or crystal vases on both your bedside tables, will heal relationships and bring refinement on a subtle level. If you use roses, remove the thorns before you put them on display. All flowers belong to the fire element and relate to the heart chakra. Flowers open the heart when they are received so they are one of the most wonderful gifts of love that anyone can give you or that you can give to someone else as a token of friendship or affection.

Best used for healing gentle love.

The combination of pink tulips and a romance candle will kindle both gentle and passionate love.

The romance candle is a special type of candle that can help to strengthen relationships. All candles have a strong and obvious fire energy. As the relationship area has earth energy and fire creates earth in the form of ashes, candles are one of the most perfect cures for this area. They have a pure cleansing energy and will give the relationship area more warmth, love, energy and freshness.

The romance candle has four items buried within its wax which are revealed as it burns. Nearest the top is a heart-shaped crystal which symbolizes passion and new beginnings. This can be hung in a window after it emerges. At the second level is a small amethyst which has the qualities of spirituality and contentment. It balances the energies of the intellectual, emotional and physical bodies. At the third level is jade, the stone of fidelity and dreams. It releases one's potential to be true and constant. Jade is sometimes used for dream solving and can help to release suppressed emotions through the dream process. To do this, place the jade under your pillow for 27 days. Finally the romance candle offers up a rose quartz which is particularly beneficial to the heart and crow chakra. It has a soft energy and is known as the crystal of gentle love. Rose quartz brings a sense of peace and calm to relationships; it promotes receptivity to the beauty of art, music and the written word; it enlivens the imagination and represents warm, tender young love. Rose quartz also instills permanence to one's loving nature. As you gently burn a romance candle, its treasures will all help improve your relationship.

Best used for bringing more passion and activity into your relationships.

A carving of the dragon and the phoenix should help your relationship to be more loving.

The dragon and the phoenix

bring different qualities to a relationship. The dragon represents the marvelous celestial male energy. He can make himself so small that he becomes invisible and can swell himself up so large that he fills the space between heaven and earth. He is the masculine guardian who defends the relationship and brings home blessings. The phoenix is the marvelous mythical empress of beautiful birds. She only appears during times of peace and prosperity and is an emblem of beauty. The phoenix does not prey on living things and she represents the beautiful, gentle and bountiful woman. Usually, the dragon and the phoenix are depicted with a pearl between them. This represents children or their love that they guard like a precious egg. A painting of the dragon and the phoenix or an embroidery, a carving on a chest or two figurines in the sitting room is very fortuitous for any couple. The dragon is too yang to hang in the bedroom.

Best used for bringing more love into your life.

Wipe the petals on your peach tree regularly to keep them free of dust.

An immortal peach blossom tree

in the far right-hand corner of your home or office will ensure a beautiful, loving marriage and a wonderful relationship that will withstand all the pressures of time. This is a long-standing Chinese tradition. "Peach blossom eyes" is the expression frequently used to describe the gaze of lovers. And people sometimes describe the confusion and pressures of first love as "peach blossom madness."

Best used for keeping a marriage or relationship strong.

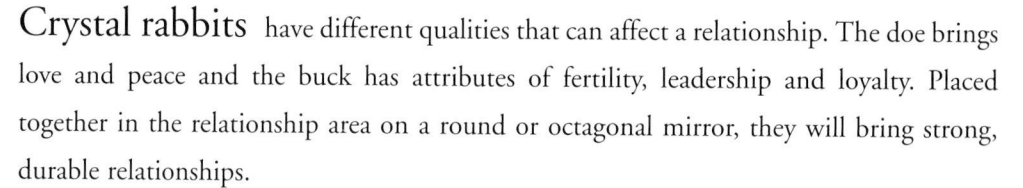

Mandarin ducks form a singular attachment for each other and are said to pine and die when separated. These beautiful birds are a symbol for material happiness and fidelity—especially if they are depicted with lotus blossoms. In China, unmarried lovers are referred to as "mandarin ducks in the dew." Place your ducks in any room in the house and they will have a beneficial influence.

Best used for when either member of a couple is thinking of wandering away from the relationship or if you are single.

A carving of mandarin ducks will help to bind ties between you and your partner.

Crystal rabbits have different qualities that can affect a relationship. The doe brings love and peace and the buck has attributes of fertility, leadership and loyalty. Placed together in the relationship area on a round or octagonal mirror, they will bring strong, durable relationships.

Best used for bringing love, peace, happiness, fertility, alertness and leadership qualities to a relationship.

A fish mobile is a popular wedding gift. The fish is an analogy for healthy sexual vigor, so hanging this mobile in the bedroom signifies the "pleasures of fish in the water." Fish also ward off evil.

Best used for bringing more passion and physical activity to a relationship in a safe way.

Hang a red lover's knot somewhere in the relationship area of your home or in your bedroom.

A red lovers' knot, an auspicious sign that was found on the sole of Buddha's foot, is described as one of the eight treasures. It signifies longevity because it swallows its own tail and appears to be endless. It also symbolizes a long, loving life uninterrupted by setbacks. The knot can be thought of as representing the Buddhist doctrine. This is that:

1 The universe is regulated by order.

2 Mankind is basically good.

3 People do wrong through lack of knowledge and from lack of example.

4 Government must lead by good example.

5 Development is inward and outward. Inward development is revealed by self-sufficiency and etiquette.

Best used for keeping a relationship strong and enduring.

Feng shui in your bedroom

Hanging a tiny crystal sphere from a silver thread in your bedroom (so it just touches the door) will slow down chi.

- The bedroom's position is very important. If it lies in the "dragon's mouth"—at the end of a long narrow corridor or lined up with the front door—it can cause problems. To counteract these, hang mirrors diagonally opposite each other to slow down the movement of chi. Also, try hanging a bead curtain from the bedroom door or suspend a crystal sphere above it. These feng shui cures will strengthen your health and improve your relationship.

- If you have a rectangular room, get a four-poster bed to create a warm, romantic and safe nest. This is particularly helpful if you are in a relationship where you seem to be drifting apart.

- Alternate your choice of bed linen among bright red, white and bright green (they have to be a shade you like) to bring more passion into your relationship. A couple who consulted me had been married for three years and, although they really wanted children, they had not consummated the marriage. I recommended this cure among a number of others and it seems to have worked because three years later I am delighted to say that they have two children!

- If you have a bed with a split in the middle, energy will gradually start to create an irreconcilable gap in your relationship. To prevent this, wrap a length of red ribbon all the way round the sides of the bed base, and lie on a queen- or king-size quilt so that you cannot feel the gap anymore. This will help to keep you with your partner and to prevent a relationship from dissolving.

- Check whether the top of your head is pointing towards your *liu sha* direction (your second worst direction, see pages 48–49) when you are sleeping. If so, it can influence a woman to stray from the relationship or be unfaithful (perhaps she is considering an affair with someone else) and may also weaken health.

  If your head is not in a bad direction and there are still tendencies towards infidelities, hang a bead curtain over the bedroom door.

Matching bedside tables with lamps help to bring harmony to a relationship. Bright red sheets will encourage passion.

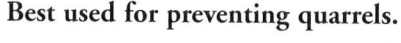

Two crystal or glass animals that represent you and your partner can help bond you as a couple. Place them on a round or octagonal display mirror somewhere in the right-hand area of your bedroom. Crystal or glass always stimulate intuition. When we are thinking clearly we make better decisions, which will bring healthier, revitalizing energy to relationships.

Best used for strengthening and revitalizing relationships.

Bamboo flutes are a useful feng shui cure if you have beams in your home. Ideally, you should not have any beams in the bedroom, over tables or in fact anywhere in the house or apartment. If possible, you should remove or conceal all beams. Failing this, the best option is to paint them white, and hang two bamboo flutes from red ribbon along one side of each beam.

Best used for preventing quarrels.

If your crystal animal is attached to its own mirror (as above), when you place it with your partner's animal, put them both on a larger mirror, so they are effectively independent but united on two mirrors.

Mirrors are a wonderful cure if your bedroom is not square, which is the ideal shape. If you apply the bagua to a bedroom that is not square, you will discover it has one or more missing areas. This can create imbalance and disharmony in your relationship. To remedy this, hang mirrors on the wall that borders the empty space; they'll make up the missing areas.

An artist I gave a consultation to had been living in an apartment where the relationship area of the whole place was missing for about 11 years. When she had originally bought the property the sellers had been in a hurry to transfer ownership because they were getting divorced. The artist had been engaged and was enjoying a lovely relationship when she first moved into the property, but within three months the relationship had ended. And she had been single ever since. We hung a mirror along the missing space (it was impossible to make up the space physically because it was a first-floor apartment) and we also used the first transcendental cure on page 70. Within a couple of weeks she met a new man, and six months later he asked her to move into his house. The cure definitely worked for her!

Best used for keeping all aspects of the relationship strong and stable.

A lamp is a symbol of fertility. In Chinese tradition, when one is placed under the bridal bed, it is called the "children and grandchildren lamp." Other lamps, known as the "all night long lamps" are also placed on each side of the bed. To encourage harmony, both the lamps should be switched off in unison for the first 27 days of a marriage.

Best used for encouraging a couple to live in harmony.

Pictures of couples are a much better influence in a bedroom than those of single people—there should be complete equality in shared bedrooms. The images do not have to be of a man and a woman, but extend to animals and birds. Even a couple walking down a single track can suggest inequality that irritates our subconscious minds. There should be two of everything—bedside tables, lamps, even alarm clocks. So make sure the bedroom is designed with equality in mind.

Best used for creating a long-lasting, loving relationship.

Healthy plants are good in a bedroom, despite any old wives' tales you might have heard to the contrary. In fact, even hospitals are beginning to allow them back onto wards. Plants absorb stress; they freshen the atmosphere and they are always growing (so long as you are looking after them!). This means that they will be activating and subtly moving energy in an upward and outward direction, which in turn prevents stagnation. So plants always have a generally beneficial and healing impact on the area in which you place them. You can use plants in the bedroom to encourage all of the above and also to soften sharp corners that can create stress and tension.

Best used for preventing illness, tensions and quarrels.

A red or pink lava lamp or astro lamp in the relationship area will help either you or your partner to stop sulking or getting a feeling of being stuck in a rut. Sulking comes from stagnation so you need to make sure that the chi is always kept moving.

Best used for preventing sulkiness.

A bead curtain hung somewhere in the relationship area will help to strengthen feelings between you and your partner when things seem difficult. If you have two doors connected by a corridor, hang a curtain to slow down the chi. Otherwise, hang one in a doorway.

Best used for strengthening the relationship with your partner.

Choose a bead curtain that complements the surrounding color scheme and is right for that bagua area.

67

A carving of a pair of cranes is an effective substitute if you cannot find a suitable picture.

A picture of two cranes has great significance. According to Chinese legend, a hard-working, wealthy mandarin once employed a poor young man as a secretary. In time, the humble secretary and the mandarin's beautiful daughter fell deeply in love. They secretly met whenever they could, knowing that the mandarin would not approve of such a match. One fateful day they were discovered and the mandarin flew into a terrible rage. He had planned a more appropriate match for his beloved daughter with a wealthy merchant. He immediately ordered a wall to be built around his daughter's house to keep her safely away from her lover and give her time to contemplate her situation.

After a few weeks he presented his daughter to the merchant, who gave her a box of fabulous jewels as a token of his admiration. But the heartbroken girl was still very much in love with the poor secretary and while her father and the suitor were engaged in conversation she escaped with her lover and the stunning jewels she had been given. They were hotly pursued by the father, who could not believe the embarrassment his daughter had caused. The young couple hid in a cottage, where they spent a few precious hours together until they thought it was safe to try to escape by boat. But they were apprehended and the lover was charged with theft of the jewels. He was executed and the beautiful daughter, beside herself with grief and guilt, committed suicide. All was not lost, however. The kindly cranes had witnessed everything and reunited them after death by transforming them into two cranes who forever soar among the celestial clouds in a state of bliss.
Best used for overcoming all problems in love, but especially those between lovers from different backgrounds.

The peony is called the king of flowers and it is believed that vibrantly colored peonies will bring romance to a single girl of marriageable age. If you are single and want to bring a partner into your life, either hang a picture of peonies, or put fresh or artificial peonies in your sitting room or just outside your bedroom door. (Remember that artificial flowers only last for about six months.)
Best used for finding your soul mate.

A picture of a pair of phoenixes is wonderful for relationships. Unlike others of its kind, the Chinese phoenix cannot self-immolate nor self-rejuvenate. It is a beautiful bird similar to an ornamental pheasant. It only appears in times of peace and humility, it eats no living things and is very gentle. I have an exquisite embroidery of a pair of pheonixes on delicate silk hung in my bedroom and, every time I look at it, it makes me feel soft and warm.
Best used for ensuring a long and compassionate relationship.

Hang an embroidery depicting a pair of phoenixes in your bedroom or anywhere in the relationship area of your home.

A special tip for lovers

If you sit facing your *nien yen* direction (see pages 48–49) when you go out on a special date you will activate romantic luck. If you really want the relationship to work, this will greatly improve your chances. It is a powerful feng shui tool and you should only use it if you are absolutely sure that you are with the right person—otherwise it can create complications for you. This direction means marriage.

Best used for finding a husband or wife.

Transcendental cures for bringing more love or marriage

- When you next go to a wedding, take nine small crystals (preferably rose quartz, amethyst and jade) wrapped in red silk fabric. Just after the ceremony, if you are a woman ask the bride to hold each crystal for a few seconds and mentally fill each with her happiness (a man should ask the same of the groom). As the bride finishes, let her drop each crystal into the red silk without you touching them. Keep them safe until it is an auspicious day. For the next few years these are November 5, 1999, November 2, 2000, November 1, 2001 and November 8, 2002. On any of these special days, take the crystals out of the silk and put them in a glass or crystal dish. Then sit the dish on the red silk and put them on your bedside table. Leave them there for the next 27 days.

- Under your bed, roughly parallel to your heart and in the space that would be occupied by your partner, place a glass or crystal figurine of one of your compatible animal signs. The ornament should sit on an octagonal or round mirror that has a red cloth beneath it. Use your sixth sense to decide which animal is the most appealing to you. For example, if you are a dragon, you might be happy with a monkey or a rat, and a monkey or a dragon would both be just as good for a rat.
  Best used for bringing in your soul mate.

- Greet someone new every day for the next 27 days. Ask nothing of them, and don't complain. Also, if you can, try to visit at least one new place every weekend to expand your horizons.

- Say 300 times a day for 27 days "I have a wonderful new boyfriend/girlfriend," or, "I am with my soul mate." You need to feel a resonance with the phrase you use and make sure you use the present tense.
  Best used for bringing in your life partner or a boyfriend/girlfriend.

Compatible animals

RAT—MONKEY—DRAGON

OX—SNAKE—ROOSTER

TIGER—DOG—HORSE

RABBIT—PIG—GOAT

Weddings

Feng shui can help to make your wedding and marriage even more perfect.

- Feng shui prefers brides to marry in cream, ivory or any off-white shade. Pure white is the color of mourning and is thought of as being dead, so it represents death to the wedding. If you really want to wear a classical white dress, make sure you include some color in your bouquet, hairpiece or lingerie.

- Releasing doves or birds indigenous to your country on your wedding day is considered very good feng shui, as is releasing any animal generally. The dove is the bird of peace, love, patience and understanding and indicates that you will not try to imprison each other within the marriage.

- There is an ancient Chinese expression, "A daughter who marries is like spilt water—she cannot look back." So as they leave the reception, the bride and groom should spill two cups of water on the road and then drive off without looking back. This means that the marriage will last forever.

- A small, round or semi-circular fan is a lucky bridal accessory. Fans are a transcendental cure and are a symbol of goodness. Traditionally, a fan is given as a parting gift to ensure a comfortable journey through life. If you don't want to carry a fan and your guests are to sit at the reception according to a seating plan, an alternative is to write their names on small, colored fans to indicate their designated places.

- When heeding the Western tradition of wearing "something old, something new, something borrowed and something blue," think carefully about who you borrow the items from. Choose someone who enjoys a happy relationship.

- Red is the most auspicious color, so if you want to give life to your marriage, incorporate splashes of red into your wedding. This could be the car, the chauffeur's uniform, your lingerie or a garter.

- It is considered very auspicious if either of your parents have died or if they can't be present for any reason. Acknowledge their absence with a red rose on your table at the reception. You do not need to set a place, simply put a rose there for each parent with the intention.

- Make a recording of the music from your wedding day—not the whole ceremony but the music of your choice. Replay this during special occasions and it will add a special chi essence.

- Confetti should consist of dried rose petals, dried lavender flowers, dried marjoram and uncooked rice. Traditionally, the maid of honor would supply the confetti. All guests would pay a small amount towards the cost because everyone should throw some. As they throw confetti, the guests should send happy thoughts for the couple.

- Getting married on the right day is of the utmost importance. The day that something is born will influence that thing forever, whether it is a person or a business, a building or a marriage. If a lucky day is chosen for the wedding ceremony, it will ensure that there are children from the marriage, and that the relationship is built on friendship and harmony. So consult an expert about which days are auspicious for you and your intended.

- To seal their love, the bride and groom should both place a glass or crystal Chinese zodiac animal that corresponds to their year of birth in the relationship area of their bedroom.

In many countries, the bride and groom exchange rings as tokens of love and to seal their marriage.

Strengthening your family

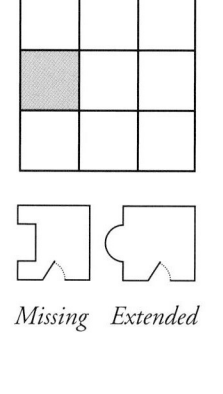

Missing Extended

Ancestors area

You will find this area in the middle left-hand side of your home or office (see also pages 16–17). It relates to your family, past and present, including your brothers and sisters. According to feng shui, we are energetically linked to our blood relatives, which means that if one member of the family goes by the wayside so does everyone else. If we fall out with our brother, it is like saying we have fallen out with one of our arms.

Whenever something happens to your family, in some way you will feel the reverberation. This link may be more obvious if you consider the families of a notorious murderer or a pop star. But if you look closely I'm sure you will see some echoes of subtle events manifesting throughout your whole family too. Perhaps everyone in the family has been depressed at the same time even though they live far away from each other. So this area is very important.

Whenever possible, try to display photographs that show members of your family together, in groups or couples.

The ancestors area doesn't just relate to our families. It also governs the health of the liver, blood, teeth and addictions and influences our relationship between people who are in a position of power over us. In addition, it relates to new ideas and inspired thought.

If this area is missing in your home, you will tend to have less vitality and enthusiasm. Family relationships may become tense or distant and you may have difficulty starting new projects.

If there is an extension in this area, it is considered lucky as there is a greater chance of success in your vocation. Family relationships will tend to be strong and healthy and you will enjoy lots of inspiration.

If you display a photograph beside a green Buddha candle, position it so that the person in the photo is looking towards the Buddha.

Quick cures

A memorial tablet or family tree should be kept in this area. Western family trees include names and corresponding birth and death dates. However, on their family trees the Chinese add the cause of death, the person's occupation and sometimes personality traits.
Best used for keeping the family close.

Photographs of relatives, past and present, can be displayed in this area. Try to have some pictures in which you feature too.
Best used for keeping the family united and strengthening your better qualities.

A green candle in the shape of a Buddha can be burned when you really want some guidance or when you want to send energy to someone in need of help. Green is the color of growth and rapid transformation. It also belongs to the wood element which energetically feeds the flame of the fire element. These candles are commonly burned in the ancestors area to send out mental or physical healing energy.
Best used for bending healing energy to relatives or friends, past or present, who need help.

A lamp shining upwards is good for alcohol addiction. Leave it on all the time; it will help to give the addict more energy and to see the light.
Best used for treating alcohol addiction.

A silk embroidery showing the 100 birds that bestow blessings and honor.

A picture of the 100 birds will ensure riches and honor till the close of life. It also brings lots of variety, flexibility, good health and an easygoing personality. Birds are considered fortunate because they care for people, bring joy and keep graves clean.
Best used for gaining long-lasting honor.

Strong hardy evergreen plants will help to strengthen the health of family members. Both a peace lily and a money plant are a good choice. When you place a plant in the ancestors area, mentally dedicate it to the member of the family who is unwell.
Best used for when someone in the family is ill.

An indoor fountain in the ancestors area of your home can help when you need support from someone in a position of power who has been blocking you. For instance, this might be a bank manager who is trying to call in a loan. A small fountain in this area will also smooth quarrels that have been carrying on for a long time. The movement of the water will unblock the stagnation. A bubbling fountain is also one of the best cures for healing an alcohol addiction. One of my clients had a husband who had been an alcoholic for many years and always refused to recognize his problem. Very soon after installing the fountain he joined a self-help group for alcoholics of his own volition!
Best used for gaining support from powerful people, for healing family quarrels or for treating alcoholism.

Shou Xing is always gentle and smiling. He will keep the whole family peaceful, safe and long lived if he is placed in the ancestors area. He appears when peace reigns and he offers long life with good health and happiness. He is portrayed holding a bat which represents the five blessings of a long and healthy life, wealth, love of virtue, fame and a natural death. In his hand he holds immortal peaches from a fabulous peach tree which grows in the palace of Hsi Wang Mu (Queen Mother of the West). She is revered by women on their 50th birthdays. The legend is that she lives in a palace made of purest gold, with walls 333 miles in circumference and bedecked with sparkling precious stones. She is escorted by two maids, one with a fan and the other with a basket of the peaches of longevity which grow in her garden. Five other girls, the Jade Fairy Maids, are part of her retinue. They represent the four principal compass points and their center.

In paintings, the Queen Mother of the West travels on a magnificent white crane and her messengers are a flock of bluebirds. Her palace stands by the lake of jewels and near it grows the fabulous peach tree that flowers only once every 3,000 years and fruits 9,000 years later. When this happens the Queen Mother of the West has a banquet at which the chief delicacy is the fruit which is served after dishes of dragons' livers, phoenix marrow, bears' paws and monkeys' lips.

Best used for strong health and peaceful family relationships.

A fish tank with nine fish placed in the ancestors area is a good cure if the health of the family is generally not very strong. This might be because it is going through a stressful time or having financial problems and you all (including yourself) need some assistance from a supportive and powerful person.

Best used for gaining support for the whole family.

A radio playing in the ancestors area can help when you need some support quickly from your guides or boss, the bank manager or your family. Keep the volume fairly low.

Best used for an emergency like a sudden need for support.

Three healthy plants that need a lot of water should be kept in the ancestors area. The constant movement of the water they require is cleansing and sends out healing energy.

Best used for any addiction.

Make sure that your plants are always healthy and are given the right amount of water. Neglected, unhappy plants have a negative influence.

Funerals

We should not think of funerals as tragic events but as being a part of life. Everything in this universe moves in cycles. As we age our bodies prepare us for the afterlife; we become thinner and thinner until we are pure spirit. Of course, it is sad for those who are left behind and even more tragic if loved ones die young, but they will be going on to the next level. We will all follow at some point, so we could view death as if people were emigrating to a distant land. At their funerals, we can send them off in a fitting way. A number of Chinese traditions can help bring good feng shui to a funeral. Here are some key traditions:

- A feng shui consultant would be employed to select a suitable burial site and to indicate the direction in which the coffin should be laid and the date on which the funeral should be held.

- If a cremation is chosen, the soul is said to wing its flight to the nether world, carried in the smoke, which is a messenger of the gods.

- If the body is to be buried, the grave must be maintained for at least four years because it is said that the Po, which is part of our spirit, will remain for that period of time. According to Taoist doctrines, the physical form of a person is the Hsing; the Po keeps the body alive and the Hun is the conscious mind. The Po and the Hun separate at the time of death, but sometimes, perhaps if the person has been murdered or dies in a sudden accident, they may remain united. When the Po and the Hun part company, the Hun leaves the body through the fontanel and goes to the nether world. The Po stays with the corpse for about four years, which is why it is important to tend the place of rest.

- The Chinese have procedures for dressing the body. A lady would have white undergarments and a new full-length overgarment of red or yellow or red and yellow (any shade of red from palest pink to scarlet and any shade of yellow from ivory to daffodil). The clothes should be made of cotton, silk or satin. Fur lining or the skins of animals should never be used. A gentleman would wear white undergarments and blue outer garments. Again no fur lining or skins of animals should be worn—even on the feet.

- The deceased's name, occupation, dates of birth and death and main characteristics would be written on a tablet. (Today, we might use a framed photograph instead with the relevant details written on the frame.) This would be placed on a table very near the coffin for the entire funeral, and then taken home where it should remain in a prominent position for 49 days. Thereafter, it should be placed in the ancestors area of the home. This tablet/photo is considered almost sacred; some doctrines say it contains the essence of the departed.

Burn some candles in memory of the departed. They have a gathering effect and will help to guide the spirit onwards.

some countries mourners are hired because the more people who attend, the more energy will be generated to help the spirit on its way.

- The loved one's favorite music should be played, not necessarily hymns. It needs to be personal and encapture the energy of the departing person.

- If they enjoyed dancing when they were younger, a dinner dance could be organized with that kind of music. Perhaps, before the music starts, a slide show and anecdotes about the person can be mentioned.

- Mirrors should be turned to face the wall or covered during the funeral and wake. Mirrors draw energy towards them and we are trying to send spirit on.

- Putting flowers on a grave is a simple way of helping the bereaved to focus their thoughts on the loved one and therefore send them some mental energy.

- Wearing an armband or a bracelet can help to bring the loved one into our thoughts. Every time we glance at it we will be reminded of that loved one and will therefore send some mental energy. This should be done for 49 days (49 is traditionally known as the number of redemption).

Happy incense, lucky money, and red, yellow and white flowers help to prepare the spirit to travel to the next world.

- Incense should be kept burning for the duration of the funeral service, preferably in a church but if this is not possible then at home. This is said to prepare a way for the spirit.

- Two cream candles should be kept burning constantly during the service to draw the departed's guides and loved ones to guide them to the next level.

- Traditionally, in every culture a wake would be held to which everyone from the village would be invited so they could send energy to the departing soul. In

After the funeral

Once the ceremony and ritual of the funeral and the wake are completed, the Chinese follow some additional traditions in the years to come. These bring the family together and provide occasions to focus on ancestors past and present.

1 A year after the death a lamp is left burning on the grave. A candle in a glass dome is best for this.

2 In China, each year around April 15, graves are repaired and tended. Then a picnic would be held near the grave of the dear departed.

3 On the anniversary of the death, it is customary to draw a picture of a present, put it in a red envelope and burn it for the deceased, so it can be carried in the smoke to the next world.

Financial focus

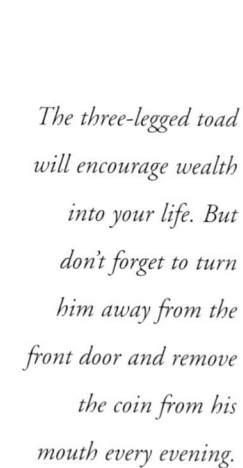

Missing   Extended

Wealth area

The wealth area of your home lies in the part of the building that is furthest away from the front door on the left-hand side (see pages 16–17). This area relates to wind, growth and communication. The energy here should be bright and fresh with the feeling of growth, curiosity and lots of movement. Your wealth area doesn't just relate to finances and luck but also to self-empowerment. Money gives us freedom so we do not have to kowtow to our boss or our partner or parents. If you are looking for a wealthy partner to take care of you then there is something lacking in this area.

We need to make our own money. As the prophet Khalil Gibran said, to be really happy we should stand side by side and not in each other's shadow. If we are to reach our full potential, neither one of the partnership should be leaning nor being leaned upon. If

The three-legged toad will encourage wealth into your life. But don't forget to turn him away from the front door and remove the coin from his mouth every evening.

Transcendental cures

If you are flat broke and want to change your energy, about once a week try to wander through the wealthiest places you can find, perhaps an exclusive hotel. Have a cup of something to drink there, and read a luxurious glossy magazine showing the most exclusive jewelry, elite cars and the best houses. Or you might prefer to visit a showroom that sells the most luxurious and expensive cars. Basically, go to the "moneyed" areas; stroll around for perhaps an hour and soak up the prosperous life energy. If you do this frequently you'll absorb new ideas and thoughts and auspicious things should begin to happen for you too. If it is difficult for you to visit affluent areas then buy luxurious glossy magazines (or borrow them from a library) that show the finest jewelry, cars and houses. If the magazines are your own, cut out your favorite images and display them in your home.

The prosperity signature can also help to attract wealth, success and renown. Your signature should be firm and clear (not necessarily discernible but the same consistency of pressure and form and not excessively complicated). It should begin and finish on an upward stroke. If you sign your name with this type of signature after making a wish 49 times for nine days, your wishes should come true.

someone is keeping you or if you are carrying someone, you inevitably lose the power to reach your potential.

The wealth area also relates to the hip, the gall bladder, impatience and irritability.

If the wealth area is missing, finances will be a struggle. Good luck may seem as if it is passing you by and there may be accidents in your life.

If the wealth area is extended, you are a very lucky person! It is extremely auspicious to have an extension here. It means lots of money, good communications and general good luck coming your way.

Quick cures

A three-legged toad, sitting on a pile of gold nuggets, can bring his owner great success and luck in money. He should be carrying a string of six ancient Chinese coins on each side of his body. According to legend, he comes from the moon. Thus, he can help his owner to achieve the seemingly unobtainable. To activate the toad god, place him within view of the front door. Every morning, place the jewelled coin in his mouth to signify that he will always deliver prosperity to you. Remove the coin and turn him to face towards the interior when you get home each evening to prevent him from becoming exhausted.

Best used for bringing in lots of money and spending it wisely.

An indoor fountain is a splendid alternative if you don't want to keep a fish tank. Not only do fountains improve your finances, they also act as natural ionizers. They create a fresh and healthy atmosphere especially in centrally heated or sealed rooms (where the windows won't open) and the fresh air aids good health. Place the fountain near the front door. If it has a spout, make sure that the water is flowing towards the house; if it flows away then it can mean money going out of your life even faster. In addition to the wealth area, other good sites for a fountain are in the children, helpful people and ancestors areas. Indoor fountains have an additional characteristic. If you live near a busy road or in a noisy neighbourhood, the gentle water sounds can create peace between the quiet of your home and the outside noises, thereby contributing to a harmonious environment.
Best used for helping you to take your power into your own hands.

The moist air from a fountain absorbs electrical pollution and creates a healthier atmosphere.

A fish mobile (opposite) will ward off evil while also bringing more wealth into your life.

Three Chinese coins on a cash box or in a till in the back left-hand side will improve profits. As with the gold I Ching coins, they need to be linked with red ribbon.
Best used for improving profits at work.

Three coins hung over a store's door will encourage money to come into the store. Hang the coins on a length of red ribbon.
Best used for increasing business.

A fish mobile or a statue of fish signifies gold and jewels filling your house to overflowing. They are also regarded as a charm to avert misfortune. Hang or place fish in the wealth area, in the hall or in your bedroom. If you have too many doors or windows aligned in a row, try hanging a fish mobile between them to change the movement of chi.
Best used for averting danger from money and bringing more money in.

Three gold I ching coins kept in your handbag or wallet are a useful cure to encourage wealth. You can also fix them onto your money-coming-in-book (bank statement or checkbook), or simply place them on top of a mirror in the wealth area. The

number three represents rapid growth. Whenever you get a grouping of three of anything there will always be growth and tension, whether it is three fish, dogs or people.

If you and your partner were to go on vacation, you are less likely to meet any new people because two is a number that is complete. But if you and your partner and your best friend were to go on vacation then there would be lots of growth and movement. One day you and your friend might go shopping and leave your partner in the bar. On your return you would probably find he had made new friends so your numbers would have grown.

Three never remains constant. There is a tension and jealousy associated with this number, but above all there is growth and movement and this is what we want for our finances. The reason the three coins must be linked with red ribbon is because red is the color of blood and thus gives life to the money, ensuring that your purse will never be empty. The dragon and phoenix on the back of the coins signify equal masculine and feminine energy. Together, they make sure that the money in your life does not get too strong and start to weaken your health.

Best used for financial growth.

Keep your money plant healthy or you will find that your financial affairs will also go into decline.

A jade (or money) plant is an excellent feng shui cure. The Chinese rank jade as the most precious stone. It should be soft, smooth and glossy just like the leaf of a money plant. The character for jade represents three (the number of growth) so to increase finances you need to look after your money plant, because within a short space of time the plant links with your energy. If the plant comes to grief then your finances may also come to grief. To increase the power of the plant, put a piece of red cloth wherever you are going to position the plant. Put a display mirror on top of the red cloth, then three Chinese coins linked with red ribbon on top of the mirror. Finally, place the money plant on top of the coins. To make this cure even more powerful, bury nine coins (of any currency) in the soil.

Best used for making your money grow.

A basket of fruit or flowers symbolizes riches. Keep the basket in the kitchen—with a mirror underneath to double its energy.

Best used for money that strengthens your health.

Goldfish mean gold in abundance. They make a marvellous wedding gift or house-warming present, especially if accompanied by a lotus flower. Fish have soothing qualities which strengthen health. They also have the power to bring good fortune and harmony. Odd numbers of fish avert evil omens. The red fish symbolize long life, the gold money, and the white spiritual growth.

Best used for bringing steady and ample finances.

A red goldfish will encourage its owner to have a long life, as well as invite wealth into the home.

One or three small convex mirrors fixed above the stove to reflect the burners and give a good view of what is occurring behind the cook are another financial cure. If cooks cannot see what is happening behind them they will tend to be more hurried and take less pleasure in creating culinary delights. The stove influences your finances, so to improve your cashflow make sure you use all the burners regularly. They energize our "money luck" and need to be used in turn to prevent stagnation. If you have four burners, the mirrors will double their power by energetically creating eight.

Best used for improving finances and harmony in the home.

A pond or lake at the front of the house will attract wildlife and cleanse and revitalize the immediate area. Water is regarded as the lifeblood of a garden. A pond will

Ponds and feng shui

You can improve finances if you are fortunate enough to have water in the wealth area of your garden. If this is not the case, you could always install a kidney-shaped pond (this is the ideal and most effective shape). The water should curve gently towards the house. Then hang a mirror to bring the reflection of the water into the house. This will encourage money into the house and should generally improve your finances. It should also bring good fortune into all aspects of your life.

make your life path more varied because it falls in the career area. As a general rule, it is beneficial to have water at the front of the house. Traditionally, however, water should not be placed to the right of the front door, as it can make the man's energy too strong and vigorous which can lead to him being tempted to have many partners. Generally, a pond or lake should be within a 30-degree area in line with the front door, but not too close to the property. If you are installing a new pond, fill it with water lilies and goldfish. For good feng shui, water should not have a large single rock, sculpture or an island in its center. Ideally, the water should be flowing towards the house or falling in a circular pattern.

Best used for bringing lots of financial opportunity.

A Chinese gold nugget or ingot has a very distinctive shape. It looks a bit like a boat and is considered to be a very lucky present. It was the currency of high-ranking noblemen and means money coming in with no effort, just floating towards you as if on the water. Try using one as a paperweight in your wealth area.

Best used for money coming in.

Place a Chinese gold nugget in the wealth area of your home or on your desk in your home office to encourage wealth to come into your life.

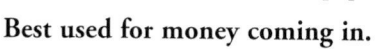

The red Chinese dragon is thought to be very lucky. Put one somewhere in the wealth area of your home to ensure financial success and good fortune.

The mythological Chinese dragon has certain parallels with the Western one in that all Chinese dragons can find or disgorge an extraordinarily precious pearl and Western dragons guard and collect treasure. There are many kinds of dragon. The spirit dragon can produce rain and the heavenly dragon protects the immortals. The red dragon guards mortals and is particularly auspicious—wherever he is there is sure to be luck and wealth.

Best used for protection and improving finances.

A bead curtain will slow down the movement of chi, if your front door and your back door are lined up together. Otherwise, it can mean money comes in and goes out equally quickly. Hang the curtain between the two doors. You could also try blocking the path by hanging wind chimes above the front door.

Best used for stopping your money rushing in and rushing out.

A whirlpool bath may help if your bathroom is in your wealth area, in which case you may be experiencing financial difficulties. It will change the flow of the chi from downward to upward thus balancing the energy—but only if you take a bath every day!

Best used for if you have a bathroom in the wealth area.

The Buddha lucky charm is a happy reclining Buddha who holds two gold ingots—one with his hand and the other with his foot. This lucky charm is said to bring abundance and joy into the home and its inscription reads, "May wealth and money pour in." Hang your charm near the front door or in the wealth area of your home or office. **Best used for bringing in wealth and lucky money.**

An eight coin book mark should strengthen your ability to fulfill your potential and use your freshly assimilated knowledge to bring you money and opportunity. **Best used for turning knowledge into money.**

The eight coins in this bookmark are linked with auspicious red ribbon and will help you to make the most of knowledge that you acquire through reading books.

The money mouse is a symbol of intelligence and loyalty. He represents industry and prosperity on account of his ability to locate, acquire and hoard abundant supplies. The money mouse is very clever and very kind. He looks after his family and does not take offense even though people are jealous of him. Place him in the wealth area.

Best used for promoting industry and prosperity.

Place a carving of the kindly money mouse in the wealth area of your home.

A money collage is another useful feng shui cure. Money has an energy all of its own. To demonstrate this point, sometimes during my seminars I silently take out nine notes of a high denomination and fix them to a wall. For the duration you could hear a pin drop because the atmosphere is so tense. Money energy is very powerful; it really does take over the whole room. Permanently fixing money in your wealth area creates more money; it represents money coming in and staying. It's not practical to stick notes of money on your walls, so this is where the money collage comes in. You will need a gold-colored picture frame and a red background. On to this, fix nine notes and an amount of coins that is divisible by three of any currency to make an abstract picture. Or you could make a figurative picture out of the money. For instance, you could draw a tree, then stick coins on to represent the leaves, and perhaps draw two or three "stick" people and use coins for their faces. Use some notes to represent the ground—and use your imagination.

Tie this tiny yellow jade ingot onto your handbag to make business meetings financially successful.

Some of my clients have made real works of art. One that springs to mind was of some fish and the whole family, including the children, got involved with its creation. Mr. and Mrs. Briggs have a pub that had been struggling for many years. Eventually, they decided enough was enough and it was time to call in a feng shui expert. When I arrived, I found the pub had a very tired, stale, depressed atmosphere that was affecting everyone. One of the things I asked them to do was to stick foreign notes and coins along the top of the bar and to encourage their customers to bring in a few coins or notes when they returned from their holidays and add them to the growing collection. They complied with enthusiasm— and the result is lovely. Within three months the place was transformed— the atmosphere is happier and livelier and the pub is much more lucrative, with the income doubled.

Best used for money coming in and staying.

A yellow jade double ingot hung on string from your handbag will ensure money luck follows you wherever you go.

Best used for important money-related meetings that occur off site.

Choosing presents

Buying a gift for a loved one can be hard work; whether we are spending $5 or $500, the stress levels are often much the same. The best way to select a present is to ask what the person wants, especially as nowadays we often live far away from our relatives, which makes it difficult to know what to give. But unfortunately they often don't even know themselves! I have compiled this list as a guideline to help you choose an appropriate gift according to a person's date of birth as dictated by their Chinese horoscope characteristics.

Rat people cannot live without passion and adventure. They are very charming and have great imaginations. Buy them something bizarre and strange that seems to have come from a faraway place. It does not have to be practical. You could even invent a story about the gift—perhaps that you dug it up from some ancient site at great risk to yourself! It could be a three-legged toad or an old ring that used to belong to a beautiful Chinese princess who worked bravely and secretly as a spy defending her people. Never let on that you bought it from a Chinese exhibition!

The rat years are:
1/31/1900 – 2/8/1901
2/18/1912 – 2/5/1913
2/15/924 – 1/24/1925
1/24/1936 – 2/10/1937
2/10/1948 – 1/28/1949
1/28/1960 – 2/14/1961
2/15/1972 – 2/2/1973
2/2/1984 – 2/19/1985
2/19/1996 – 2/6/1997

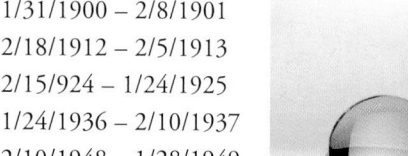
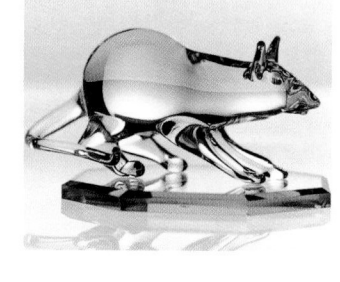

Ox people are patient and hardworking. They cannot live without contact with nature. They feel most at home when they are outdoors, especially if they have found a spot unknown to others. Generally, they love hiking, plants, flowers, and items made from natural materials. So you could fairly confidently buy them a money plant. To activate the plant you need to bury nine coins of any currency or denomination in the soil. Hiking boots or socks, an unusual orchid or boxes of bedding plants are also appropriate presents. If none of these appeal to you, a membership of an environmental group—perhaps a local botanical gardens—would be an excellent present.

The ox years are:
2/19/1901 – 2/7/1902
2/6/1913 – 1/25/1914
1/25/1925 – 2/12/1926
2/11/1937 – 1/30/1938
1/29/1949 – 2/16/1950
2/15/1961 – 2/4/1962
2/3/1973 – 1/22/1974
2/20/1985 – 2/8/1986
2/7/1997 – 1/27/1998

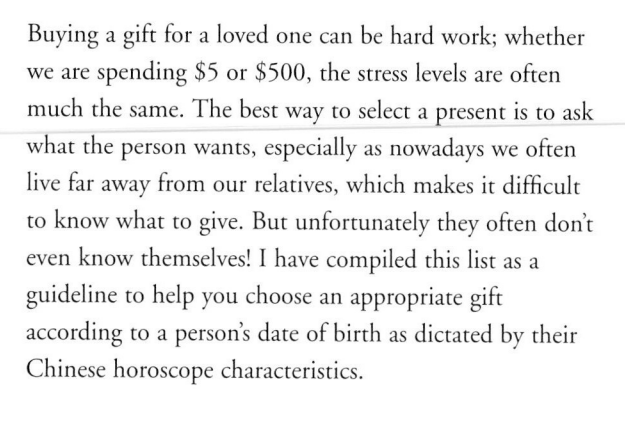

Tigers are loyal, active, courageous, enthusiastic and generous. They cannot live without the unforeseen. If your partner is a tiger, be ready to follow wherever he or she leads. You will find yourself in some extraordinary situations, but you must keep up your energy as there will be no respite. Tigers love to solve your problems, so they might like a voucher to a murder mystery weekend. They like to hunt and compete and they are always active, so they will be keen to go to any social activities, from car racing to kite flying. You are quite safe to choose any activity-based present. If you would like to buy them something to keep, a carp pen pot is a symbol of martial attributes because of the carp's ability to swim upstream and win—so this would make a great practical present.

A carp pen pot helps anyone to be a better leader but is particularly good for a tiger.

The tiger years are:
2/8/1902 – 1/28/1903
1/26/1914 – 2/13/1915
2/13/1926 – 2/1/1927
1/31/1938 – 2/18/1939
2/17/1950 – 2/5/1951
2/5/1962 – 1/24/1963
1/23/1974 – 2/10/1975
2/9/1986 – 1/1/1987
1/28/1998 – 2/15/1999

Rabbits are discreet, prudent and honest. They adore intimate gatherings around a fire—preferably while a storm is raging outside. Rabbits are very sensual so they might like some rich, quality bed linen or cushions. A soft warm robe, slippers or perfume are also suitable. Rabbits are attentive and faithful friends, hospitable, warm, refined and full of delicacy so a gift associated with entertaining, like a bottle of champagne and fine glasses, would be appreciated. The rabbit was not made for revolution so a gift of a figurine of Shou Xing, who is gentle and smiling and only appears during times of peace, would be a good present to ensure their lives are tranquil. Or give rabbits a pair of small fu dogs to protect their home.

The rabbit years are:
1/29/1903 – 2/15/1904
2/14/1915 – 2/2/1916
2/3/1927 – 1/22/1928
2/19/1939 – 2/7/1940
2/6/1951 – 1/26/1952
1/25/1963 – 2/12/1964
2/11/1975 – 1/30/1976
1/29/1987 – 2/16/1988
2/16/1999 – 2/4/2000

Dragons are active, dynamic and brilliant. They cannot fail because they cannot conceive of that possibility. Dragons are young at heart and they adore gifts that will fascinate and make them laugh. My mother is a dragon and I have rarely seen her as amused as when she was given a gift of a battery operated trick dog lead that made a barking noise. She and my aunt roared with laughter as they walked down the street with this barking dog lead and an "invisible" dog. They don't like practical

things. Another great present would be a red dragon. Legend says that he can make himself so small that he becomes invisible or he can swell until he fills the space between heaven and earth and he will bring your dragon friend great good fortune.

The dragon years are:
2/16/1904 – 2/3/1905
2/3/1916 – 1/22/1917
1/23/1928 – 2/9/1929
2/8/1940 – 1/26/1941
1/27/1952 – 2/13/1953
2/13/1964 – 2/1/1965
1/31/1976 – 2/17/1977
2/17/1988 – 2/5/1989

Snakes are reflective, wise, alert, clever and opportunistic. They cannot live without pleasing others. If you love a snake immediately resist him. He will hate it but you will gain his respect. A present that a snake will like must cost a great deal—something with a designer label whether it be a handkerchief or an outfit. Or give a snake a rare book or work of art or some discreet but expensive jewel. The snake believes in the minimum amount of effort for the maximum amount of gain so a gift of a set of three gold I Ching coins linked with red ribbon to bring him money luck would be appreciated.

The snake years are:
2/4/1905 – 1/24/1906
1/23/1917 – 2/10/1918
2/10/1929 – 1/29/1930
1/27/1941 – 2/14/1942
2/14/1953 – 2/2/1954
2/2/1965 – 1/20/1966
2/18/1977 – 1/26/1978
2/6/1989 – 1/26/1990

Horses are noble, enthusiastic and enterprising. They cannot live without being supported and encouraged. Horses are always worth listening to, and are sensitive romantic poets who will tell you how much they love you with talent and conviction. Male horses love to travel and enjoy exercise, so you could give them camping or sports equipment, or maybe a ticket to an exciting destination. Female horses like to be spoiled, so a weekend at a health spa or an exotic location (as long as it involves a plush hotel) would go down well. A crystal mobile would make a fabulous present because it will strengthen the horse's intuition and make him or her more dynamic.

The horse years are:
1/25/1906 – 2/12/1907
2/11/1918 – 1/31/1919
1/30/1930 – 2/16/1931
2/15/1942 – 2/4/1943
2/3/1954 – 1/23/1955
1/21/1966 – 2/8/1967
2/7/1978 – 1/27/1979
1/27/1990 – 2/14/1991

Goats (or sheep) are adaptable, gentle and easygoing. They cannot live without beauty. Goats are not very good with finances so a gift of money would make a nice present that will always be welcomed. A fine painting or a rare and delicate object would also be accepted with delight, but goats have impeccable taste and will spot an imitation immediately so make sure the gift is genuine. Another lovely present for your goat friend would be a membership to a gallery, but it will need to be near to home or workplace. Because of the goat's unstable finances, a fish mobile which signifies gold and jewels filling your house to overflowing would be an excellent present.

The goat years are:
2/13/1907 – 2/1/1908
2/1/1919 – 2/19/1920
2/17/1931 – 2/5/1932
2/5/1943 – 1/24/1944
1/24/1955 – 2/11/1956
2/9/1967 – 1/28/1968
1/28/1979 – 2/15/1980
2/15/1991 – 2/3/1992

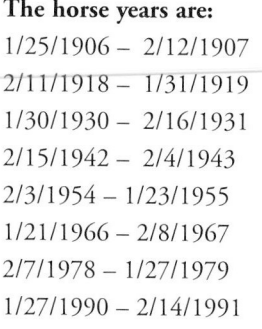

Giving someone (especially a goat) a gift of chocolate coins in numbers of eight or nine symbolizes riches coming and makes a lovely present.

Monkeys have very sharp minds; they are ambitious and gifted in everything they do. All doors are open to the clever monkey. They love to be adulated and cannot live without movement and the exchanging of ideas or discussion. Monkeys detest feeling excluded or ignored. They like to transform things and to succeed where others have failed. Give them a book on feng shui. They will understand and assimilate the information instantly and start to transform their lives and yours for the better. Or, if you prefer, give a monkey some truly fabulous cloth to make into something beautiful. A dragon-headed turtle will bring in lots of new beginnings and opportunities for the hungry monkey and a magic set will fascinate a young one.

The monkey years are:
2/2/1908 – 1/21/1909
2/20/1920 – 2/7/1921
2/6/1932 – 1/25/1933
1/25/1944 – 2/12/1945
2/12/1956 – 1/30/1957
1/29/1968 – 2/16/1969
2/16/1980 – 2/4/1981
2/4/1992 – 1/22/1993

Roosters are hedonists and they need to be appreciated. They are obliging and courageous but they are a little vain and sometimes preoccupied with appearances so they would like something that is going to make them shine and stand out in a crowd. A stunning dress, sweater or tie will do very nicely; a new sports car would be even better. Roosters cannot live without admirers. They are wonderfully romantic and will shower you with love and affection. They are hardworkers and the Chinese say that a rooster could find an earthworm in the desert if he has a mind to. So to make his life easier, a gift of an indoor fountain would be helpful to his luck, or a celestial dragon pen stand.

The rooster years are:
1/22/1909 – 2/9/1910
2/8/1921 – 1/27/1922
1/26/1933 – 2/13/1934
2/13/1945 – 2/1/1946
1/31/1957 – 2/15/1958
2/17/1969 – 2/5/1970
2/5/1981 – 1/24/1982
1/23/1993 – 2/9/1994

Dogs are loyal, faithful and generally unselfish. They cannot live without tenderness, and they like to look after things that are weaker than themselves. The dog will never be unfaithful—it is just not part of his nature. A good Christmas gift for a dog would be a mascot, perhaps a cuddly toy of a dog, horse or a tiger (these three animals form a tri-harmony). Or you could give them a protective amulet like a mayan ball or even a real pet (but make absolutely sure they really want a pet first). To be happy, the dog generally needs to have something to look after. Dogs love children and a gift of the globe of fertility which should be placed in the master bedroom would be a lovely present if your dog friend is childless.

Pigs are honorable, tolerant, persevering and steady but sometimes they lack a competitive spirit. They cannot live without love and beauty. Pigs spend their money generously as soon as they receive it, but always manage to be prosperous. The pig will love anything you buy and will be really happy that you just remembered. Their favorite place is without doubt their home, so you could buy them anything beautiful for their house or garden. Pigs also enjoy good food, so luxurious morsels from homemade fudge to a luxury hamper will delight them. A small peach blossom tree ornament in the master bedroom represents immortal love which is very important to the pig, so this would make a truly wonderful present.

The dog years are:
2/10/1910 – 1/29/1911
1/28/1922 – 2/15/1923
2/14/1934 – 2/3/1935
2/2/1946 – 1/21/1947
2/16/1958 – 2/7/1959
2/6/1970 – 1/26/1971
1/25/1982 – 2/12/1983
2/10/1994 – 1/30/1995

The pig years are:
1/30/1911 – 2/17/1912
2/16/1923 – 2/4/1924
2/4/1935 – 1/23/1936
1/22/1947 – 2/9/1948
2/8/1959 – 1/27/1960
1/27/1971 – 2/14/1972
2/13/1983 – 2/1/1984
1/31/1995 – 2/18/1996

Christmas

Applying feng shui to Christmas can generate seasonal cheer and make holiday celebrations and gatherings more enjoyable. The following ideas should help to make your Christmas a happy, less stressful occasion.

- Hang garlands at a "smiling angle," with the ends pointing up to create a small swag. Decorations that have ends hanging down generally bring the energy down too and can make us subtly sad. Things that are hung so they "lift" will subconsciously make us smile.

- Use plenty of green. There is often lots of stress around Christmas, because there is so much fire energy. Pine green is a cooling color, so plants and evergreens will cool the atmosphere and promote peace and good feelings. Green also absorbs the fire energy that is created by Christmas lights as well as the warmth from lots of people gathered in a room. It is a soothing color that will tone down and balance anything colored red.

Candles have a very gathering effect and create a warm and pleasant atmosphere, so burn some each evening.

- Angels and cherubs are lucky symbols to have around you. They fill the room with good will, peace and a fairy-tale atmosphere.

- Make sure everyone (including house guests) places something on the Christmas tree so that they put their own personal energy into it to make the gathering more linked.

- "Heed the time limit, the five colors blind" is a traditional Chinese saying that means too much color, sound and activity can have a numbing effect upon us. Too much food and color will exhaust the family, so don't put the decorations up too early (unless you are going away for Christmas). Use images of water or wintry scenes to cool the atmosphere down and subconsciously create more harmony and balance.

- A round table is the most harmonious choice for Christmas. It will encourage the conversation to flow because no one will be sitting in a dominant position.

- If you have a rectangular table, don't put husband and wife or any long-established couple at opposite ends. This is a position of conflict and can lead to tension. It is as if they are both firmly on opposite sides. One partner could sit at the head and the other on the long side one or two places away for one meal. For the next meal they should switch places.

- The table decoration needs to be the brightest thing in the room to create a focal point and prevent the conversation from splintering off. Place a round display mirror in the center to strengthen intuition and place two or more short candles on top. Arrange cut crystal animals round the candle so they look as if they are gathered round a campfire (the candles). Each animal should represent a member of the family, so that even absent relations will be there symbolically. Make a daisy chain of little pink or yellow flowers to encircle the mirror. Flowers belong to the fire element and open the heart; pink represents love and yellow represents lively conversation.

If possible, hang Christmas lights in a tree outside and fix an appropriately colored wreath to your front door.

- Vary the centerpiece each day to subtly change the vibration of each meal and help to prevent any stagnation. Use plain pink or cream tablecloths to compensate for all the color and brightness.

- If relatives are staying with you, place a photograph that was taken of them with you on a happy occasion on a bedside table in their room. It will make them feel really welcome and part of the family. If you don't have such a photo, use this opportunity to take one.

- Try to go for a walk every day, otherwise with all the food, fire, bright things and so many people, tension and tiredness can build up. After you have come in, sip a warmed drink. Use gathering herbs like ginger, star anise, nutmeg and cinnamon heated in red wine.

Choosing the right garland

The best color for a garland depends on which direction your front door faces.

- On a south-facing front door, hang a green garland with red decorations.
- On an east-facing door, hang a green garland with blue decorations.
- On a southeast-facing door, hang a blue garland with green decorations.
- On a southwest-facing door, hang a predominantly red garland.
- On a north-facing door, hang a garland that is mainly silver, metallic blue and/or gold.
- On a west-facing door, hang a white and gold garland.
- On a northwest-facing door, hang a white, gold or yellow garland.
- On a northeast-facing door, hang a red and yellow garland.

Health care

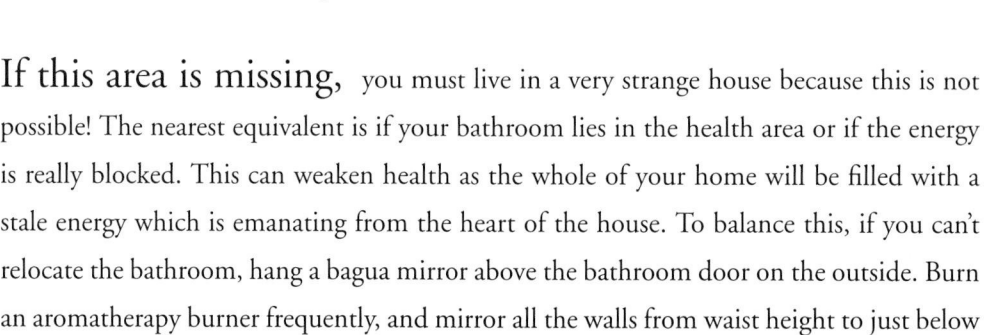

Health area

The area that relates to health is found in the center of your home and it generally includes the hall and stairs (see also pages 16–17). This area relates to all aspects of health but particularly the central areas, the nervous system, the spine and the stomach. It belongs to the earth element and if there are any problems here they will have a ripple effect in all areas. The center of the house, which is often the hall, is comparable to a river feeding energy into all the other rooms. Traditionally, there would be a chimney or courtyard in the center of the house through which fresh air would circulate.

If this area is missing, you must live in a very strange house because this is not possible! The nearest equivalent is if your bathroom lies in the health area or if the energy is really blocked. This can weaken health as the whole of your home will be filled with a stale energy which is emanating from the heart of the house. To balance this, if you can't relocate the bathroom, hang a bagua mirror above the bathroom door on the outside. Burn an aromatherapy burner frequently, and mirror all the walls from waist height to just below ceiling height (use a solid sheet of mirror so there are no joints).

If this area is extended, you will have a very large courtyard in the center of your home. This will turn your rooms into long corridors and this will create division between the occupants.

Quick cures

Bamboo symbolizes youth because it is evergreen. The Chinese expression "May his name be preserved on bamboo," translates as "May he be preserved forever." Bamboo is also seen as being gaunt like an old man and when the wind blows it is said the plant bends in laughter. So bamboo represents a healthy long life. Grow a decent amount in the garden. **Best used for keeping us flexible in old age.**

Bats are regarded in Western culture as sinister characters associated with the dark underworld. But in feng shui bats have few competitors as a symbol of good luck, health and happiness. Traditionally, five bats are shown together and they represent the five blessings. These are a long life with a natural death, riches, peace, virtue and fame. They also symbolize the five virtues, namely piety, uprightness, trust, knowledge and etiquette. Hang your five bats in your health area or in the fame area.

Best used for making you more temperate and wise, thus strengthening your health.

A spiral staircase can be damaging to health, particularly if it is in the center of the house (it represents a "drill" through the heart) and if it doubles back over itself completely. To heal the potential threat, thread green rope or an artificial plant through the banisters or up the pole in the center to stop the staircase from being a heart-piercing weapon.

Best used for strengthening all aspects of health but especially the heart.

A Buddha lends an atmosphere of serenity and happy contentment. He reminds us not to be too greedy or to work too hard. Your figurine should be made from stone, wax or china and placed in the hall. Buddha's birthday is May 8, so this is a particularly auspicious day to light a candle to Buddha and ask for any special requests.

Best used for strengthening health and coping with stress.

As with all religious icons, never place a statue of Buddha on the floor. He should be in a raised position and always treated with respect.

Cut flowers freshen the general atmosphere of a room. The combination of red and yellow is one of the most auspicious. Avoid red flowers in a blue vase.

Red and yellow flowers placed in a glass or crystal vase in the health area are a useful and simple cure. Use fresh flowers when possible, or keep artificial flowers clean and dusted (and clean them thoroughly or throw them away after about six months).
Best used for strengthening the stomach and the digestive system.

A crystal butterfly symbolizes a man in his seventies and represents happiness. Butterflies dancing among flowers also symbolize long life and immaculate beauty. Giving a gift of a butterfly is another way of saying to someone "I hope you live to be at least 70 or even 80 years old."
Best used for keeping us agile and flexible.

A statue of a crane is a symbol of longevity. He is often depicted with a pine tree, a tortoise, a mushroom or a deer (which are other symbols of long life). Two cranes flying up towards the sun express the wish that the recipient may rise high. The crane represents wisdom and he is supposed to be an emissary of the gods. (Sometimes cranes are depicted

on coffins if the deceased was considered to be very moral and was extremely long lived.)
Place a statue of the crane in the health area of your house or garden. If you haven't got a
statue, you could hang a picture of a crane.

Best used for strengthening the mind in old age.

The magic ting is a bowl that usually has the image of a dragon in relief on its base. *It takes years of*
After it has been filled with water, a practitioner rubs the handles rapidly until the water *practice to master the*
leaps up, forming a wave pattern. At the same time, a sick or elderly person should hold *art of using a magic*
the sides of the bowl. The vibration emanating from the bowl strengthens and balances *ting, so its use is best*
their internal chi. *left to a qualified feng*

Best used for balancing your energy. *shui consultant.*

The lotus flower is one of the eight treasures. It reminds us that beauty can grow out of ugliness, and so a picture or image of one is beneficial if you are depressed and feel generally gloomy. **Best used for combating depression.**

Kuan Yin, loosely translated, means, "She who observes and pays attention to all prayers." She is the Chinese goddess of mercy. This radiant and gracious goddess usually holds her hands in a heart-healing *mudra* (hand gesture). She wears a rosary and flowing white gowns which represent purity. She also holds a vase that symbolizes perfection and contains the essence, or *ling*, of children waiting to come into this world. Legend says that she can grant the desire of those who truly wish to have children. She helps those who seek relief from pain and is known as the one who will save those who are lost and hurt, no matter what they've done. Most of all, Kuan Yin is the protector of children and women. Place her in the middle right area of the kitchen, in the children area or near the front door. The 19th day of the moon in March, July or August is the best time to ask for children and protection or to move her to a new place. To establish the 19th day of the moon, count 19 days after the night of the new moon, counting that as the first day. **Best used for protecting children from temptation.**

Small wind chimes are an invaluable aid to strengthening your health. Sickness inevitably comes through our front doors each year and, according to feng shui, the energy of disease belongs to the earth element. Earth gives birth to metal and thus weakens the virulence of the illness, so you will be more likely to stay healthy. But if you do become ill, you will recover more quickly and your illness will be less debilitating. Windchimes also act like a gentle alarm bell, warning you if someone is coming into a room. **Best used for warding off illness and anxiety.**

Pine trees strengthen a man's health. Placing a picture of pine trees or putting a pine bonsai in the helpful people area will energetically bring the vibration of the pine into the house. **Best used for strengthening a man's health.**

Health area tips

- Long narrow corridors create bad health because they squeeze the chi and create tension, leading to stressful quarrels and division. Hang mirrors diagonally opposite each other in the corridor to expand the area energetically.

- Any room at the end of a long narrow corridor is said to be in the dragon's mouth, which is a dangerous place to be! Chi rushes too quickly along the hallway to the end room carrying unstable energy. This can cause illness and things happening out of control, so hang a bead curtain to slow the chi.

- If you suffer from constipation and a change in diet hasn't helped, the first step is to have a de-cluttering session. After you have done this, putting a lava lamp in the health area may solve the problem.

Shades of yellow and red or healthy skin tones should be used in the center of the house to ensure that health is strong and energy is flowing in a positive way to all areas.

Best used for promoting movement in a subtle way to prevent the slowing down of the organ functions.

The deer symbolizes healing and longevity. Shou Xing wore a deer skin so that he could collect precious deer milk medicine from the immortal deer in the hope that it would restore sight to his blind parents. The deer is thus a symbol of strong health.

Best used for encouraging a healthy old age with all faculties remaining strong.

Burning an aromatherapy burner will have a revitalizing effect on your health if it is used in the center of your home. It doesn't matter what type of aromatherapy oils you use as long as you like their fragrance.

Best used for revitalizing all aspects of health.

Jade is regarded as an extremely precious material. More valuable than diamonds or gold, it is considered to bestow immortality. Jade emerges from a mountain as liquid (this is true) and solidifies after 10,000 years (which is a Chinese way of saying a very long time). Apparently, if it is mixed with the right herbs it will return to its liquid state (which is probably true). When it is drunk, jade is said to produce an elixir of life that will bestow a very long and vigorous life (but not immortality). A jade item is best placed in the center of your home. Or you can wear jade jewelry or keep a piece of jade in your pocket as a talisman, especially against being thrown from a horse. Travelers can also carry jade in their pockets to protect them against illness.

Best used for longevity and to protect health while traveling.

The Chinese regard jade as very precious. Even small pieces have protective qualities.

A bright lamp in the center of the house will have a similar effect to fire energy. This lamp should be used daily; it may be easier for you to keep it on a timer switch, so that it turns itself on if you are not at home.

Best used for strengthening the general health of the whole household.

Your hall should be bright and uncluttered to keep the atmosphere fresh and healthy throughout the whole house.

Best used for maintaining good health and preventing tiredness.

Transcendental cures

- Every compliment you are paid is like a gift. We rarely value these precious gifts of happy energy and their restorative value is soon lost. Buy a jade green notebook and write in it each compliment you remember anyone giving you and every new one you receive. Then you will have a string of jade compliments with the power to uplift and improve your personal chi. Read the list whenever you feel depressed or you need a boost to your energy.

- Every time you look in a mirror say something positive about yourself. If you subconsciously criticize your looks, the mirror will magnify that criticism and create a black cloud of negative energy that will depress you and others in the house. So be

positive; you might say something nice about your posture, how clever you are, the shiny hair you have, your lovely genuine smile, the flattering color you are wearing, or how you like your beautiful eyes. Then you will surround yourself with a positive energy that will be reflected and magnified back. You and everyone around you will feel happier and any depression will be eased.

- If you were once slim, have put on weight and now want to lose it, put a picture of your former self on the fridge. This will subconsciously remind you of how slim you can be again, whereas a picture of you looking plump will psychologically enforce that you are overweight.

Keep your hallway free of clutter, with nothing piled on the floor. This will benefit your health and give you more energy to complete daily tasks.

Handbags

You can apply the principles of feng shui to almost any item—even a handbag or a briefcase. First of all, look in your handbag. What is inside? Is it full of candy wrappers, crumbs, scraps of paper with phone numbers and scribbled notes? Or is it neat and orderly? Are you carrying everything but the kitchen sink with you or is your bag light, with only the bare essentials?

The first principle of feng shui is eliminate clutter. The aim is to create a smooth, steady flow of energy, allowing good things to come into our lives and for us to move on when the opportunity arises. If we have too many belongings it is almost impossible to be tidy and organized. So, here are some simple steps to having a clutter-free handbag. If you follow them all, I can guarantee that your handbag will be neat and tidy.

- After you have chosen and purchased your handbag you need to select several matching or complementary smaller bags for the things you will carry in it. You might need one for your makeup, another for tickets, receipts and other pieces of paper, and a third for aspirin, sewing kit, etc. In short, buy as many little bags as you need in order to compartmentalize the contents of your bag.

- Zipped pockets within the bag should contain only one thing—such as change for the meter or a little notebook and pen so you don't have to search around and you will remember what is in there.

- Ideally, you need more than one handbag, but not too many, or you will end up adding to the clutter. Basically, you should have one for daily use. This should be as small as you can cope with—the bigger the bag, the more you will be tempted to put in it. You will need a larger bag for overnight or day-tripping and, finally, you need one for evening wear.

The choice of color influences our personality. According to Chinese astrology, each color will have a subtly different influence upon each individual depending upon his or her date of birth. But as a general rule, individual colors have different associations. It is usually quite safe to use our intuition as a guideline when selecting colors—but be aware of what those choices might be saying about you.

BLACK has the essence of power and money. It is the color that absorbs the most and will give you more power. If you are feeling a bit insecure or tired you will probably be drawn to black. It belongs to the water element and therefore represents money. If your handbag or briefcase is adorned with gold, silver or any metal, it symbolizes great riches.

RED has the essence of life. A woman using a red handbag is looking for excitement, passion and adventure. Red is the color of blood, life and passion, so you need to be a very lively person to be happy with this color.

GREEN has the essence of evolution. A green handbag represents travel and growth, so this is a good color for a purse because everyone wants money to grow. Someone with a green handbag is looking for a relationship that involves lots of outdoor activity. Green suggests that you want to travel and may easily become jealous.

BLUE has the essence of truth. It is a spiritual color that represents truth, honesty, caring and a conservative, supportive approach to life. Someone with a blue handbag is looking for a caring, long-lasting traditional relationship.

PINK has the essence of healing and love. A woman with a pink handbag is looking for romance and a life like a fairy tale. Pink is the color of healing and has the most feminine energy.

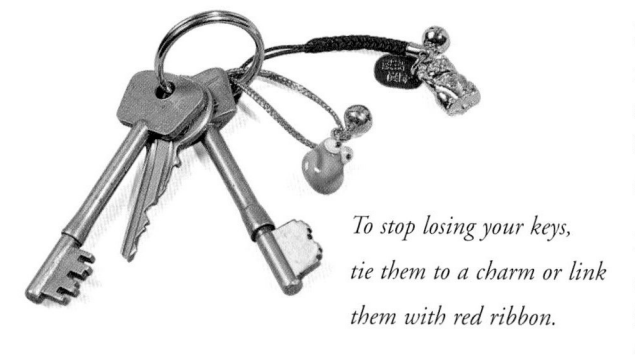

To stop losing your keys, tie them to a charm or link them with red ribbon.

YELLOW has the essence of intellect and control. It is the color that was reserved for Chinese emperors and is associated with control. The color represents wisdom, intellect and the academic world. A woman with a yellow handbag is looking for an intellectual relationship.

ORANGE has the essence of health. This color is the most expressive and stimulating of all. It is connected with communication, expression, vitality and enthusiasm. A woman with an orange handbag will love life, is easygoing and is inclined to be nurturing.

BROWN has the essence of stability and is conservative and steady. If you are very scattered and tend to behave impulsively, then brown is a good choice. But if you are already quite conservative, it can turn you into a plodder. Brown is associated with the earth and all that is secure, solid and permanent. A woman with a brown handbag is probably reliable, traditional and practical.

WHITE has the essence of purity. A woman using a white handbag is open to suggestion. She is often a little gullible and may be looking for a someone to take care of her. White is really a non-color, which simply radiates all the other colors. In China it is the color of mourning because it is a lifeless color, with no blood.

ANIMAL PRINTS carry some of the vibration of the animal. A woman with this type of handbag is looking for a primal relationship.

GOLD OR SILVER can strengthen your intuition and represents ostentation, money and fame. A gold or silver handbag has a metal energy and is therefore not a good choice for an everyday handbag. Someone with a gold handbag is quite self-contained and is looking for attention.

The shape of a handbag

Vibrations are contained within the shape of a handbag, so always consider this when you are making a choice.

- Someone with a triangular bag is looking for tension and movement. They do not want comfort but to move out of their current situation.

- A bag in the shape of a rhombus (narrower at the top and wider at the bottom) is known as a money bag. It will help you to save and attract money.

- A crescent-shaped, floppy bag will make you more relaxed, esoteric and spiritual, but be aware that it may also make you less efficient.

- A bag with a square shape will help you to complete things. It is a safe, stable, conservative, and no-nonsense shape.

- A round handbag represents money and movement, so it is a good choice if you want to attract these.

- A rectangular bag represents growth and movement. If it is a vertical rectangular shape it represents rapid movement into the unknown (unproved knowledge). If it is horizontal, it means rapid movement along the known (the field of already learned and proved knowledge). So a rectangular bag can help you to expand your horizons.

Make sure that your handbag and the little bags match or are coordinated.

Friends and travel

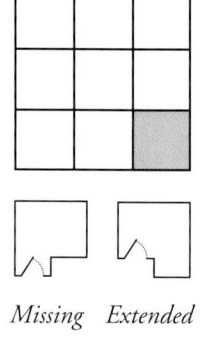

Missing   Extended

Helpful people area

The helpful people or benefactors area is found in the right-hand area just inside your front door (see also pages 16–17). This area has the most masculine energy in the whole of the house. It influences our tendency to travel and therefore when we are planning to move house it is useful to balance this area. The helpful people area is also associated with charity and philanthropy. When it is in balance, it emphasizes our qualities of generosity and fairness. When it is out of balance, we can become too attached to things and find it difficult to forget and forgive easily.

This area should be disciplined and organized. The facet of health it influences is the large intestine, which is otherwise known as the great eliminator. It belongs to the metal element. The helpful people area enjoys a dynamic relationship with the wealth area so if there are some problems here, we can "power" up the wealth area to help restore balance.

If this area is missing then it is difficult for a man to be really happy. His health may not be so strong, and it is unlikely that he will be "boss" of the house. The man will tend to spend a lot of time away from home, which can lead to relationship difficulties. If this area is missing, you may also experience difficulties with employees or colleagues. Finally, you will find it difficult to go on vacation or move to another home.

If this area is extended, it is very positive feng shui. Inhabitants will have lots of friends and support, their finances should be quite strong and they will be protected.

Quick cures

The Qilin or unicorn is the embodiment of justice and princely virtue. He can apparently discern the guilty from the innocent (to whom he is benevolent) by piercing people with his fleshy horn, which will not harm the innocent but is a powerful weapon against wrongdoers. The unicorn has been used historically throughout the West and the

Use a Qilin incense
burner to increase
virtue in your life and
those of your friends
and family. It will
also bring you closer
to the spiritual world.

East outside buildings of importance, like the Houses of Parliament in London, where he is used as a symbolic guardian outside several entrances. According to legend, he makes a noise like a musical bell, has the body of a deer, the tail of an ox, the hooves of a horse and a single fleshy horn. He will eat no flesh, can walk on grass without crushing it and his nose emits two clouds of purple mist. Burning the unicorn's horn apparently confers the ability to see into the future so he is often portrayed as an incense pot. The smoke that exudes from it is a symbolic link between ourselves and the spirits. Place a unicorn in the helpful people area or the children's area.

Best used for cultivating honor and virtue and encouraging them in yourself and your friends.

An empty metal vase or bowl brings new beginnings and opportunities for the male members of the family.

Best used for a man who needs to start a new career.

Place an empty metal vase in the helpful people area if a man needs encouragement to embark on a different line of work.

A bowl of apples will make the environment of your home more calming and peaceful.

Apples are a token of peace and therefore make a wonderful symbolic gift for a friend. A bowl of fresh or golden (everlasting) apples will bring peace to your home.

Best used for creating a peaceful atmosphere.

Put up inspirational images to make things happen in your life. Use postcards you have received or perhaps pictures cut from magazines.

Pictures of distant lands that you would like to visit should be hung in this area if you want to travel and go on vacation more than you do now. If you want to move to another home, stick up cards or pictures of the sort of house and area you would like to live in. Whatever we put around us we tend to recreate. As this area relates to travel and movement, images like these will have a greater influence on us if hung here.

Best used for if you never go on vacation or have been meaning to move but cannot seem to achieve it.

A picture of the three friends hung in the helpful people area will bring desirable friendship qualitites into your life. The picture shows the magpie, who is bright, quick witted and observant; bamboo, which is flexible and durable; and plum blossom, which is long lived, sincere and wise.

Best used for bringing friends with the above qualities.

The bear symbolizes man. He stands for strength and courage and is regarded as a potent charm against robbery. He is also associated with the stellar constellations of the Great and Little Bear (father and son). A picture or a crystal figurine of a bear in the children area will encourage the coming of a son. An image of the bear can be used to strengthen the health of the man of the house or to draw him closer if he is spending a lot of time away from home.

Best used for protection, for encouraging a son and for strengthening a man.

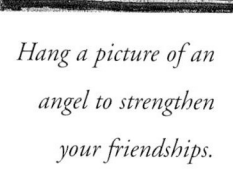

Hang a picture of an angel to strengthen your friendships.

Pictures of angels and St. Francis of Assisi will encourage more positive energy for yourself and your friends.
Best used for promoting friendships and philanthropy.

An eagle is a symbol of strength. If depicted perched on a pine tree, this is a suitable gift for an older man as it wishes him the strength of the eagle and the longevity of the pine. An eagle on a rock signifies a man who fights a lone battle. The eagle has a negative influence on a woman's energy, so place him in a man's office.
Best used for helping a man to win in work.

A fish tank with black or silver fish inside will prevent stagnation and bring more activity into your social life.
Best used for increasing your social life.

Fruit or snacks, like candies and nuts, served in a metal, glass or crystal bowl will generally encourage visitors and members of your family to make themselves at home and encourage giving and receiving. This will promote the right kind of energy in this area.
Best used for promoting friendships.

Place bowls of candies in the helpful people area to make friends feel at home when they come to visit.

On a photo of your house write SOLD and place this in a black, white or black-and-white frame. Look at it every day for a few minutes. Never voice that it is difficult to sell your house.
Best used for selling a house.

A mirror hung opposite the entrance to the room which falls within the helpful people area, or opposite a window in this area, will bring more energy and more activity to that facet of your life.
Best used for increasing your social life.

A stereo or audio equipment positioned in this area will activate good luck and belongs to the metal element.
Best used for giving your social life a boost and helping you to sell a house.

For a good atmosphere

Try to use some blue, yellow and white in this area. These colors will strengthen the room energetically because this is a metal area and these colors harmonize with metal. White represents cleanliness and strengthens intuition, yellow is gathering and blue represents finances and the masculine.

Away from home

- If you are staying in a hotel or you are a house guest and there is a mirror opposite the bed in your room, hang something over it to make sure that you can't see your reflection.

- To make sure business meetings are successful and lucrative, put a three-legged toad god opposite the door to your room.

- Burn a candle in the relationship area of your room if you are having a romantic weekend away or if you are trying to win the support of someone.

- Burn a candle in the fame area if you are away because you are having an interview for a new job.

- Keep a piece of jade in your pocket or wear a piece of jade jewelry to protect you while you are out and about.

- If there is anything negative outside your room, hang a bagua mirror in the window shining towards the sha.

- Burn an aromatherapy burner in the helpful people area if you need support.

Wearing a jade pendant will help to protect you when you are away from home visiting friends or traveling on business.

109

Dinner parties

When planning a dinner or supper party, check that all your glasses are sparklingly clean, with no chips or cracks, and that they match.

One of my regular clients is a single gentleman whom I will call Mike. He was planning an important dinner party for three friends, one of whom he had had a crush on for a couple of years. He thought the feeling was mutual but somehow they had not managed to get together. So after checking and fine-tuning his house, we started to plan the all-important dinner party. The following list of tips are from suggestions that were made so that Mike's romantic evening would go well and they should help anyone to help kindle romance:

For a romantic dinner party

- Use a square table. The square belongs to the earth element and is consequently a very safe and stable shape. Diners tend to sit for ages at a square table.

- Seat the object of your affection furthest into the room with a good view of the door. People seated near the door tend to leave the party first, and they can become unsettled from the movement behind them.

- If you can, position your intended sweetheart in his or her *nien yen* direction (see pages 48–49). (We couldn't because we didn't know her date of birth.)

- I suggested that Mike sit opposite the woman rather than near the kitchen door. This seating arrangement would mean that he would be more inclined to get involved in the conversation rather than being constantly distracted by the food cooking in the kitchen. I also orientated him so that he was utilizing his *nien yen* direction to make him feel more relaxed.

- We didn't want the other couple to be too comfortable because ideally we wanted them to leave before the woman. So we sat the person who generally made the decisions with his back to and nearest to the door (whoever sits here will generally leave first).

- I then sat in the position his "lady love" would be taking and looked around. Right in front of me was a huge painting in very strong colors of a lady surfing. She was portrayed with her back to the room surfing at top speed into the distance—away from the room. The psychological influence would be to make her subconsciously think of leaving! So we replaced the picture with one of a beautiful woman in Victorian lace clothes reclining on a chaise longue with a handsome man sitting beside her looking as if he was about to kiss her. It was a very tasteful, romantic painting. Then we hung a picture of two horses galloping in harmony together (all these pictures we raided from Mike's daughter's room!) and the room started taking on a more intimate atmosphere.

- We chose a warm yellow fabric tablecloth, from his selection. Red or pink would have been just as good as these colors open up the heart and bring warmth to the table. It is important to avoid strongly contrasting stripes, checks or jarring abstract designs.

- Next we needed to create the table decoration. We placed a round display mirror in the center and put two nightlight candles in a sparkly candleholder on the mirror. Around the candles we arranged cut crystal butterflies and rabbits. There were two reasons for this placement. First, the candles, mirror and faceted crystal made a very bright focal point that helps to stimulate conversation. Second, we tend to imitate whatever is going on around us, so by arranging the animals in a friendly fashion it would encourage Mike and his guests to gather around. If crystal animals don't appeal, you could make a decoration simply by arranging pieces of faceted crystal from a chandelier with *diamanté* items on a mirror—but the animals do give a better result psychologically.

- Then we made a chain of little pink rosebuds to place around the edge of the mirror. Flowers belong to the fire element and open the heart. We chose pink to activate romance rather than passion.

- We checked the china and made sure it was all matching and nothing was broken or chipped.

- We chose music that was subtly romantic, happy or gentle and flowing. Discarding songs like "I want to wash that man right out of my hair," in favor of songs like, "Words are all I have to take your heart away." Music can affect our mood instantly and can move us to tears or dynamic foot tapping!

- Next we prepared an aromatherapy burner with jasmine, rose and ylang ylang for romance and added some orange for zest. Mike lit the burner in the hall 15 minutes before his guests were due to arrive.

Later Mike called me to say that the dinner went just as planned and that he and the woman have established a relationship. Let's keep our fingers crossed for them.

General rules for entertaining

- A round table is the best shape if you are planning a supper for a group of people. It means everyone is equal and able to participate with no particular person dominating. There will be lots of movement and so conversation will flow smoothly.

- Again, as in romantic dinner parties, it is better to use a fabric tablecloth because it is warm and soft and subtly helps people to relax.

- It is very important to choose comfortable chairs. Wrought-iron chairs may look beautiful but they are not very practical and need plenty of cushions.

- Always use candles because they have a very gathering influence. Whenever you light a candle it will become a focal point and draw everyone a little closer. But the candles must be short, otherwise they will create a barrier between diners. If you have a tall candelabra, experiment by placing it as a centerpiece; you will see whether it will create a division between diners opposite each other. If so, this will stifle conversation.

- Fortune cookies are a perfect ice breaker. They will stimulate conversation and always go down well.

- Use a sparkly centerpiece, similar if not identical to the one I have suggested for a romantic dinner party. This time the garland of flowers should be much bolder and brighter—try using orange nasturtiums, for instance.

- Pictures are important. A group gathering would benefit from pictures of a happy party of people dining and laughing and having fun perhaps at a picnic, someone's home or in a restaurant.

- If you know your friends' dates of birth, try to position them so they are seated in their auspicious directions (see pages 48–49).

- Don't position teapots, jugs, coffee pots, knives or serving dishes with handles so that they are pointing directly at one of your guests or they will create a subtle tension.

- Don't use cracked china or glasses. Discard these items straight away because they are irreparable. Superstition says that they will affect your livelihood and that they symbolically cut the mouth.

- Make sure your choice of music is happy and fairly lively to stimulate conversation, but don't have the volume so loud that people can't hear each other.

Remember that one of the three secrets to happy relationships is eating together—so happy eating!

Children and fun

Missing   Extended

Children area

You will find the children area of your home in the center right-hand side of the property (see also pages 16–17). This area relates to our children's successes and failures; their health and energy, and whether or not we will have any children. It also influences our pets and hobbies. That vintage car in the garage can be referred to as "your baby"! All the things that we do for fun and get excited about emanate from here. The area relates to joy. If there is no laughter in our lives then we need to see what is going on in this area. The children area influences the health of your lungs, skin and mouth.

If the area is missing, there will be little joy and life may seem like hard work. It can be difficult to conceive children and it is difficult to spend your money on any pleasurable activity. Or you may find that you only spend money on practical things like repairing the roof.

If the area is extended, you are indeed lucky. It means you are more likely to experience joy and pleasure. Money should come to you easily without you having to work hard for it. You will be sociable and enjoy good intuition. It will help to make it easier to conceive children and you can expect to maintain good relationships with them.

Quick cures

A crystal elephant (below) and a crystal bear (opposite).

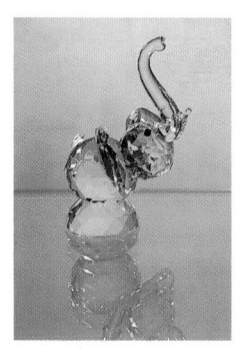

Crystals are one of my favorite cures. They bring brightness and light and thus will bring more energy, brightness and light to both you and your children. One of my clients asked me to visit because her daughter was depressed. In the children area of her home, we hung round faceted crystals in a window and placed crystal creatures on a display mirror. These were a swan for serenity, poise and contentment; a bear for kindness, warmth and stability; a squirrel for ingenuity and adventurousness; a mouse for quick wits and charm; a doe rabbit for happiness, love and peace; a seal for fun and laughter and an elephant for wisdom. The children area does not just relate to children, joy and pleasure, but also to the lungs. These govern depression so if the area gets stagnant we get depressed. The goal was to create lots of movement and sparkling happy energy—and the result was a happy child. **Best used for a depressed or morose child.**

A cherry tree has energy that will strengthen all feminine energy. Within nine months of the birth of a baby girl, a cherry tree should be planted in the garden. Ideally, the baby should be present to encourage the tree's support through her life.

Best used for supporting a girl.

A couch in warm earth colors that is really deep and comfortable will bring more softness to your children and comfort and quality to your life.

Best used for if you are very stressed and you and your family are finding it difficult to relax.

Burning a seven-day candle for the first seven days of your baby's life is an ancient custom that is thought to help to protect against the seven early diseases.

Best used to prevent illnesses in a child.

A red shirt would traditionally be given to a newborn child on the first day of his or her life. The child does not have to wear or even see the shirt but the garment would be placed in the children area of the house. The red color is very strengthening and it pulls the child's energy into the home. The material also strengthens his energy.

Best used for strengthening a child's health.

Red is the color of life, which is why a red shirt is said to protect the health of baby boys and girls.

The globe of fertility is a helpful feng shui cure. The globe is hollow and made of porcelain (symbolic of an egg) that is fashioned in the likeness of the mushroom of longevity. It sits inside a crystal globe and is decorated with a hand painted image of Kuan Yin, the goddess of mercy. She wears flowing garments of white that symbolize her purity, and sits on a lotus flower floating on moonlit water. A little boy sits near her with palms pressed together. He is asking her to find him a mother and father. Kuan Yin is the protector of children and women. She protects the home and the household from misfortune, ill-health and brings the blessing of children.

Best used for protecting health, the household and increasing fertility.

Kuan Yin is depicted on the globe of fertility and offers protection to mothers and their children.

A pine tree can strengthen masculine energy. If possible, plant one in the garden before a baby boy is nine months old. The tree's energy will support him for the rest of his life. Try to plant the pine in the child's presence and state your intention.

Best used for supporting a boy.

A fish tank with seven fish will energize children, make them less stressed and generally improve their fortune. If you don't have any children, the tank will make you inclined to have more fun and ensure that money comes in without too much effort.

Best used for bringing more fun into your life and getting easy rewards for the children.

One feng shui cure for childless couples is to plant a mainly pink or purple fuchsia in the children area of their garden.

A fuchsia that is predominantly purple or pink and is planted in the children area of the garden will strengthen a relationship and make it more bountiful.

Best used for creating children.

A Buddha with children is a perfect gift for a couple who want children.

A Buddha with children

helps to bring children into your life. He also helps to keep you young in mind. Place him in the west of your home or in the children area. Never sit him on the floor; this shows a lack of respect for religious beliefs and opinions.

Best used for bringing children into your life.

A red material ball

that is stuffed with feathers represents many things connected to fertility. Traditionally, a woman of marriageable age would invite suitors to present themselves below her balcony. She would then throw down a red ball and the man who caught it would become her husband. The best day for this ceremony is the 15th day of the moon during September. (Count 15 days from and including the first night of the new moon.) A red ball was also fastened to the roof of the litter which bears the bride to the home of her bridegroom. The reason it is a symbol of fertility is that the circular shape represents an egg and bright red is the color of healthy blood and gives life to children in the marriage.

Best used for increasing fertility.

Pictures of children or baby animals

placed almost anywhere in your home will help to bring children into your life. They can be postcards, posters or fine paintings, but it is better not to use photographs of children you know because they will have a very strong vibration of being someone else's. Whenever I go into someone's house, I know what is going on by spending a few minutes looking at the pictures on their walls. A few years ago, I visited a charming family in Wales. The 17-year-old daughter's bedroom was full of pictures of babies and I mentioned to the mother that her daughter would be having children soon. The woman was shocked. Less than nine months later the young girl became pregnant, and her mother called me to tell me that I had been right. But all I had done was read the writing on the wall. What does the writing say on your walls?

Best used for bringing children into your life.

The globe of the 100 children is a powerful cure. Traditionally, the master bedroom in the Chinese Emperor's palace would be decorated with images of the 100 children on the royal coverlets, the walls and even the screens to encourage royal descendants. Each child symbolizes fertility and is handpainted on a mushroom-shaped porcelain globe, which is finally encased in pure crystal. Place the globe in the children area. If you haven't got a globe, a painting or embroidery of the 100 children hung in your bedroom will also encourage pregnancy.

Best used for bringing children into your life, having fun and strengthening your children's intuition.

Place a globe of the 100 children either in your bedroom or in the children area of your home.

A small indoor fountain will be beneficial in the children area. It must be made mainly from metal if you want to have children. If you just want more fun, it can be made of pottery.

Best used for becoming pregnant and having more fun.

The lucky money pig is used to bring luxury and financial security to mother and children. Place the pig in the children area of the nursery or the house.

Best used for making sure mother and children want for nothing.

The wealth area is an alternative place to put a carving of a lucky money pig.

Christenings

Using feng shui for christenings or naming ceremonies can bring babies good luck that lasts all their lives.

- Use your child's good luck symbols. You may ask whether luck really exists but it certainly does. If it didn't, how can we explain how some people can win the lottery time and again? Statisticians would say that this is almost impossible to achieve, but it happens. Some people are showered with luck and seem to lead charmed lives.

  We all have lucky charms or symbols which connect on an invisible level to good fortune. According to feng shui there are three types of luck. Heaven's luck is related to your date of birth and influences your character. You cannot significantly change this luck but you can modify it (remembering that we are destined to have good years and bad years). Earth luck is about making sure we are in the right place at the right time and doing the right thing. Finally, there is good old-fashioned luck which is when we make the right decision by chance.

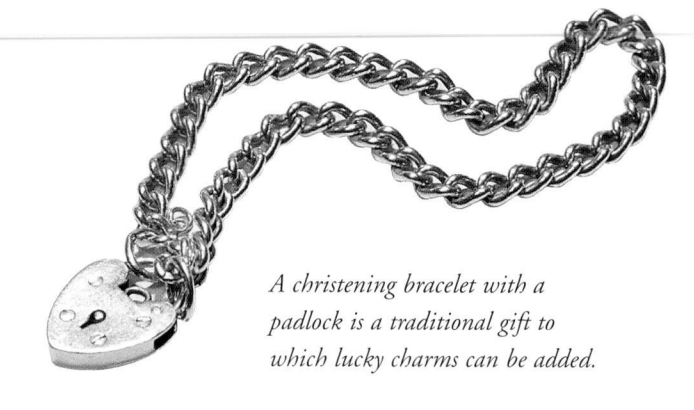

A christening bracelet with a padlock is a traditional gift to which lucky charms can be added.

- Lucky charms encourage fortune to shine upon us. There are certain shapes and types of things that will have a harmonizing effect on our psyche. Depending on the Chinese year your child is born (see pages 88–91), use his or her charms as decorations or illustrations on place settings. The lucky charms are:

  FOR THE RAT, a piano and a harp

  FOR THE OX, a teapot and a bell

  FOR THE TIGER, shoes and scissors

  FOR A RABBIT, a cat and a boat

  FOR A DRAGON, a key and a pearl ring

  FOR THE SNAKE, a turtle/tortoise and a bird

  FOR THE HORSE, a duck and a hat

  FOR THE GOAT/SHEEP, a lamp and a sea creature

  FOR THE MONKEY, the moon and a mask

  FOR THE ROOSTER, a purse or a money clip and a bottle

  FOR THE DOG, a violin and a butterfly

  FOR THE PIG, a swan and a fairy

Plant a cherry tree to bring good luck to a new daughter.

- Choose a color for the event that supports your child, pink for a girl or blue for a boy. Ask all the guests to sport something in that color, even if it is only a tie, socks, a corsage, a scarf or some jewelry.

- Choose godparents who will support your child. The list below identifies the animals that will support and complement your child.

  THE RAT CHILD—a dragon, monkey or rat

  THE OX CHILD—a snake, rooster or ox

  THE TIGER CHILD—a dog, horse or tiger

  THE RABBIT CHILD—a goat/sheep, pig or rabbit

  THE DRAGON CHILD—a rat, monkey or dragon

  THE SNAKE CHILD—a rooster, ox or snake

  THE HORSE CHILD—a dog, tiger or horse

  THE GOAT/SHEEP CHILD—a rabbit, pig or goat/sheep

  THE MONKEY CHILD—a dragon, rat or monkey

  THE ROOSTER CHILD—an ox, snake or rooster

  THE DOG CHILD—a tiger, horse or dog

  THE PIG CHILD—a rabbit, goat/sheep or pig

- Give each of the godparents a photograph of their godchild with the baby's full name, date of birth and the names of all the godparents written on the back or on the frame itself. This will help the godparents to remember the child's birthday and link them together more closely.

- Choose the godparents early on, as they should help you to prepare for the event. Decorate invitations to the christening with symbols of lucky charms and pictures of animals that support your child's Chinese zodiac animal (see pages 88–91). For example, if you have a daughter born in the year of the rat, the invitations should be pink, perhaps with deeper pink writing. They should be decorated with her lucky charms (pianos and harps), dragons and monkeys and, of course, rats to represent herself.

- Your parents (the baby's grandparents) should give you or plant in their own garden a cherry tree for a little girl or a pine tree for a little boy. The trees should be dedicated to the child's happiness and health; their energy will give the child more emotional and physical strength.

- Christening bracelets are similar in concept to the tiny, ornate padlock that the Chinese traditionally put around a child's neck to link the child symbolically to life. Christening bracelets often have a padlock as well as charms. If your child is a rabbit, suitable charms would be a cat, a boat, a rabbit, a pig, and a goat/sheep. Charms for a goat would be the same animals and a lamp and a sea creature.

- When choosing a child's name, it can be very beneficial to select an unusual one. A traditional name will not have as fresh a chi essence as an unusual name. People will remember an unusual name more easily and look more closely at the child, which will give him or her more energy to help them to succeed in life and stand out in a crowd. Another thing you might want to take into consideration is that if your surname begins with an "S," for example, choosing a name beginning with "R" would be beneficial because this letter precedes "S" in the alphabet. Energetically, there will be a smooth progressive chi flow.

- Whatever you call your children will have a strong influence on their destiny. If a child has a soft fluffy name like Candy, she will tend to be more sweet; if his name is Butch, he will tend to be a bit tougher. Each time children hear their names part of their subconscious is influenced by what they are associated with. They are also likely to be teased by their contemporaries in a way that is in keeping with the meanings of their names.

It is a good idea to tell godparents, family and anyone attending the christening what gifts you would like for your child to prevent clutter from accumulating.

Increasing knowledge

Missing   Extended

Knowledge area

The area that relates to knowledge within your home is at the front left-hand side of the building (see also pages 16–17). This area is a white earth area and relates to study and learning, as well as to our interest and ability to assimilate new information and ideas. When we are in balance we are nonjudgmental. We approach situations with an open mind and examine new "things" before we draw conclusions. We are less naive and gullible and are open and flexible. Because this area relates to study and knowledge the atmosphere should be quite still and steady (when we rush around we have no wisdom). So gathering colors like yellows and oranges will work well in this area. Traditionally, it is known as the area that spirits come in through (because it has a very yin atmosphere). Changes in this area can influence your stomach, pancreas and hands.

If this area is missing, it can affect your hands and the people living here will be less interested in new things. They tend to be inflexible in their views and not interested in new perspectives. It can also be difficult to conceive in a house that has a missing knowledge area.

If this area is extended, the building will be a good shape for a monastery or convent. But for most people, it will create an environment that is too yin. It can lead to the occupants being preoccupied with spiritual learning and growing apart from their contemporaries. And it is not easy to make money or be taken seriously in this house.

Check through your bookshelves to see whether you need to keep all your books. If they are cluttering your shelves, pass them on to a new home.

Quick cures

Books bring a quality of stillness and respect to an area. They also contain the vibration and enthusiasm of their authors which you bring into your home with each book. This can create a lively intellectual atmosphere (depending on what sort of books you have). Go through your books frequently to prevent stagnation and dust from gathering.
Best used for creating stillness.

Comfortable chairs that are well upholstered with plenty of cushions are a much better choice for a room in the knowledge area than wood or metal seating. This part of your home should be soft, warm and welcoming.

Best used for if the occupants are too inflexible.

An office or desk sited in the knowledge area will encourage you to achieve good results because the atmosphere is conducive to study. If you do have an office in this area, make sure that your telephone, fax machine and computer all face one of your auspicious directions. The points where electricity flows in are more important than the position of the equipment.

Best used for studying proficiently.

A real or gas effect fire is an effective cure in the knowledge area. It will increase the energy in the room, making it easy to study and helping you to assimilate the information fully.

Best used for helping you to study.

A statue of a tortoise, especially if made of stone, symbolically and physically slows down the movement of chi, because life goes at a gentle pace for the steady tortoise. It breathes extremely slowly and may even live to be 150 years old. If you do not have a tortoise, you could use a collection of rocks or a heavy stone or concrete statue to achieve a similar influence (but not a figurine "in flight"). Use these artifacts if there is too much movement in this area, or if you find it hard to stay in one place.

Best used for if you are finding it hard to study and be generally still.

Convex mirrors can help if you are studying, perhaps for an exam, and need a cure to help you to remember your notes. Buy a red ring binder file and fix nine small (about 2 inches in diameter) mirrors on the inside front and back covers. The mirrors will shine inwards towards the notes you have prepared and give them more power.

Best used for getting the most from your studies.

Cures for your phone

For a cure to make your telephone ring, place the phone on a round or octagonal mirror that is sitting on a piece of red cloth the same shape and size as the mirror. Underneath the phone place symbols of the 12 Chinese zodiac animals in a circular design. If you want to get the absolute benefit from this cure, you can also tie nine pieces of 1-inch-long ribbons to the telephone cord. Also, make sure that the telephone cord (the one coming from the socket in the wall) is approaching from your *nien yen* (relationships) or *sheng chi* (money and power) direction (see pages 48–49 to find out your best directions).

A comfortable chair (opposite) will make you more flexible and a fire (below) will help you to learn.

The five extraordinary walnuts have 100 of the cleverest men who have ever lived engraved on each walnut. They are a valuable feng shui cure. It is said they will give you access to these great minds and that the cleverest men will devote all their energy to solving your problems. It is best to keep all the walnuts together in a group of five somewhere in the knowledge area of your home or office. However, if you are going to an important business meeting, you can carry just a single walnut in your pocket to ensure that it all goes well.

Best used for increasing acumen.

Keep the five extraordinary walnuts together in a wooden bowl.

Rugs or carpet should always be used in preference to bare wooden floors. Wood has too much movement and in this area can create an unstable vibration.

Best used for making the right decisions when things are changing.

Choose fitted carpets or loose rugs in colors that harmonize with the other furnishings in a room.

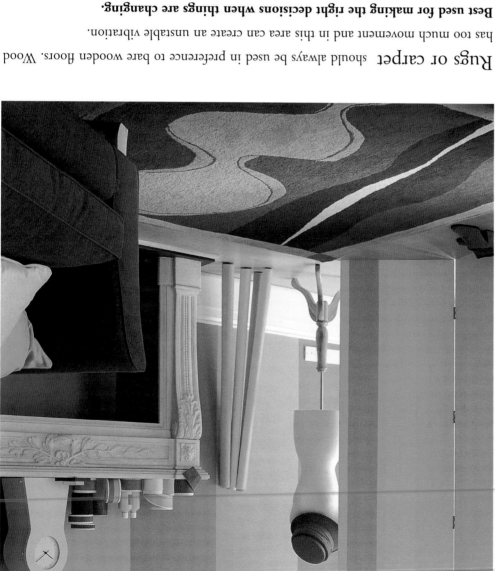

A **bell** symbolizes ideas, clarity and mental movement. Placed in the knowledge area, it is a useful cure if you tend not to be interested in new ideas and find it hard to get motivated.
Best used for coping with change and new projects.

The sound of a bell will help to clarify your thoughts when you need to come to terms with a new project or accept changes in your life.

A **Buddhist bell** displayed in the knowledge area will help to increase your morals.
Best used for promoting high ideals.

A **glass animal** that corresponds to your Chinese year of birth (see pages 88–91) placed in the knowledge area is a useful cure if you want to strengthen your intuition and increase your knowledge.
Best used for strengthening intuition.

A figurine of Shou Xing brings his owner a long, happy and peaceful life.

Four heavy stone objects or stones, one placed in each corner of the knowledge area, will help anyone who has put so much energy into spiritual studies that they have lost touch with the reality of everyday life and have become "ungrounded." If this applies to a teenager or someone who only occupies one room within a house, the four stones can be placed together in the knowledge corner of that person's room.
Best used for making someone more in touch with the material world.

Shou Xing is a gentle and smiling feng shui cure to help increase your knowledge. He is often known as the god of the North Star because he originated from the stars. According to legend, when he appears, peace will reign. He offers long life filled with knowledge, good health and happiness. He is portrayed holding a bat (heavenly rat) which is always colored red and represents old age, wealth, health, love of virtue and a natural death. Shou Xing also holds fruit from the fabulous peach tree that blossoms once every 3,000 years and fruits only once every 9,000 years. He is said to confer longevity, wisdom, peace and happiness.
Best used for acquiring wisdom.

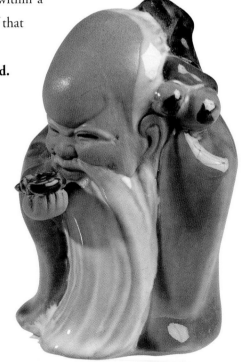

Using feng shui in your car

A green car is good for some drivers and bad for others. The chart opposite shows which colors to choose or avoid.

Feng shui can be applied to your car by using the bagua (see pages 16–17). First of all, you need to know where the "front door" or mouth of chi is within the car so that you can orientate the bagua the right way up and identify the relevant areas. The source of energy is the engine so this is the equivalent of the mouth of chi and the bagua template should be overlaid so that the engine falls into the career area. The location of the gas cap indicates what the gender of the car is. If it is on the right hand side (as you look at the car from the front) it is feminine; if the cap is on the left the car is masculine. Assuming the engine is at the front:

- the hood relates to the career area;

- the front right-hand side (passenger position) is the helpful people area;

- the front left-hand side (driver's side) is the knowledge area;

- the rear passenger right side is the children area;

- the rear passenger left side is the ancestors area;

- the far left relates to the wealth area;

- the far right relates to the relationships area;

- the center relates to the health area.

- Wherever scratches or dents occur will indicate if there is a sensitive area in your life. So, for example, if you scratch the far left side of the car, financial problems may be looming, so drive carefully.

- The center of the car should always be kept clean, uncluttered and fresh. This area relates to health and needs to have a smooth, fresh, healthy flow of energy.

- Hanging a mayan ball from red ribbon from the rear view mirror of the car will contribute to protecting against accidents, car thieves and general negative energy. This is a very old cure. Mayan balls work on the same principle as witch balls, which look like large Christmas tree decorations. Witch balls are so called because they are reputed to keep witches away—a poetic way of saying that they deflect negative energy.

    Mayan balls are always hung in cars from red ribbon or thread, because red is the color of healthy blood and gives life to the cure. They are hollow silver baubles, $3/4$ inch in diameter, with a small bell inside. One of my clients was moving to a new house in a direction which meant she was at risk for accidents for the next couple of years. So I recommended that she hang a mayan ball in her car. Sure enough, during the next year the mayan ball dropped off the rear view mirror three times because it had deflected negative energy. Since then she has not had any more trouble because the danger of accidents has receded. But she still keeps a mayan ball hanging from the rear view mirror to keep her safe.

- Keeping cushions in the car is good for keeping passengers calm. Cushions are associated with protection and comfort, which is why people often hug a cushion when they are feeling vulnerable.

- Playing audio books or calm, soothing music contributes to safer driving. We tend to drive in time with fast music, which can be dangerous.

Depending upon your year of birth, some colors will be better for you than others, and these can be applied to the car you drive. Below is a list of the very best and the very worst colors for you personally. This is according to the Chinese calendar which runs from the Chinese New Year's in early February. So if you were born in January you will belong to the previous year. For example, someone born in January 1988 should look up 1987.

If you were born in:	Best color	Worst color
1909, 1918, 1927, 1936, 1945, 1954, 1963, 1972, 1981, 1990, 1999	silver	yellow
1910, 1919, 1928, 1937, 1946, 1955, 1964, 1973, 1982, 1991, 2000	green	blue
1911, 1920, 1929, 1938, 1947, 1956, 1965, 1974, 1983, 1992, 2001	red	green
1912, 1921, 1930, 1939, 1948, 1957, 1966, 1975, 1984, 1993, 2002	cream	red
1913, 1922, 1931, 1940, 1949, 1958, 1967, 1976, 1985, 1994, 2003	white	red
1914, 1923, 1932, 1941, 1950, 1959, 1968, 1977, 1986, 1995, 2004	red	turquoise
1915, 1924, 1933, 1942, 1951, 1960, 1969, 1978, 1987, 1996, 2005	blue	silver
1916, 1925, 1934, 1943, 1952, 1961, 1970, 1979, 1988, 1997, 2006	black	gold
1917, 1926, 1935, 1944, 1953, 1962, 1971, 1980, 1989. 1998, 2007	red	green

If your car is not the best color, simply add some items of that shade inside the car.

Future and fame

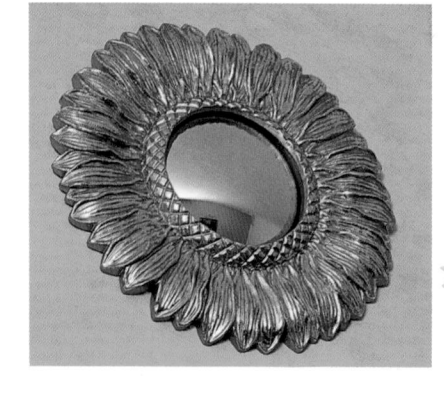

Missing   Extended

Fame area

Before you can make any adjustments, you need to establish where the fame area is in your home. This area is found at the center back of the house (see also pages 16–17). The fame area relates to our future and progression through life. It impacts upon any promotion we are likely to receive, enlightenment, and how people see us in the community. If the area is in balance you will be able to progress rapidly up the career ladder, will enjoy a good reputation and will be well liked.

If the area is missing, you can get stuck. There may seem to be no progression through life and you probably can't decide what you want to do. A missing fame area may also make you very sensitive to what other people think.

If the area is extended, you should find it is easy to get a promotion. It is also more likely that you will become famous and people will know your name and business within the community though you may not have met those people. You will tend to enjoy a good reputation.

Quick cures

A convex mirror with a golden frame in the shape of a sunflower can help you achieve fame.

An ordinary large-framed mirror (convex is stronger) hung in the fame area will put you firmly in the future. The mirror will capture light (which belongs to the fire element) and will expand your future plans, ideas and opportunities.
Best used for winning a promotion.

A sunflower or star-shaped convex mirror is an effective cure if you want to become famous or if you want a special boost. I use this cure myself whenever I need some publicity for my books and it has not failed me yet! Hang the mirror in the fame area.
Best used for achieving fame.

The phoenix on its own symbolizes the coming of wish-fulfilling opportunities that bring success and prosperity and hurt no one. When the phoenix is placed with the dragon, she energizes relationships, but for fame she needs to be on her own because the dragon weakens her.

Best used for wish-fulfilling opportunities connected with your career or dreams for your future.

Happy incense is special incense that smells of violets. It should be burned regularly in the fame area to make everybody happy.

Best used for cheering you up.

Lao Shou Xing, Fu Shinn and Lu Shin are three gods who relate to the future and should be placed in your fame area. Lao Shou Xing will keep the whole family peaceful, safe and long lived. Fu Shinn is known as the god or spirit of good luck. He holds a scroll which will attract good fortune towards you and ensure a lucky star shines wherever you walk. Lu Shin is known as the spirit of happiness and holds a *ru-ly*, which means that 10,000 things will come smoothly to you. He will encourage prosperity into your life. These gods are known by many names because they were originally mortal and had different names then.

Best used for general good luck.

The three gods who will traditionally bring you a long life of good fortune are (from left to right) Fu Shinn, Lao Shou Xing and Lu Shin.

- If this area in your home only has narrow windows and is fairly dark, it can restrict opportunity. To cure the problem, boost your career and speed enlightenment, put mirrors along your windowsills and ledges to draw in more opportunity.
- If someone is trying to take you to court, remove all mirrors, lights and plants from this area. In their place put some yellow or brown stone, pottery or concrete objects.
- If you have a delicate heart, place lots of strong, green, healthy plants here.

A treasure map is as delightful as its name. Make this picture with a cornucopia of elements that you would like to bring into your life and be very specific. Ideally, you should create a treasure map that balances all facets of your life. For something relating to your work, if you would like to be a TV star, a picture of the latest television set might be appropriate. For your relationships, put a picture of an idyllic couple. To strengthen your family relationships, use a photo of your grandparents, parents, and any other relations. To represent your finances you might write down a large sum of money with a picture of your dream car, house and maybe some jewelry. For your health, add a picture of an athlete. To activate a full social life, you could include a picture of a group of friends dancing or having fun. If you have always wanted a horse, put that in. For your personal development, a picture of books or someone meditating would be good. Basically, add something to represent all your desires and hang the map on a wall.

Best used for bringing whatever you want into your life.

Plants are perfect for sustained and steady growth. Especially beneficial are hardy red flowering plants like geraniums.

Best used for steady and sustained growth.

Windmills that children usually play with can be a useful cure. Use red, green or gold windmills and stand them in the earth of a window box outside a window in the fame area. As the wind blows them in different directions, they will activate huge amounts of chi.

Best used for gaining a promotion.

A crystal mobile combines the elements of fire and metal. Whatever the element destroys brings "wealth" to the area, so if you use metal in the fame area (which is a fire element area—fire melts metal) it can create abundance to that facet of your life. Hanging a multi-faceted crystal mobile in the window will help your ideas for the future come to fruition. This is a specially good cure if you are an inventor or a creative "ideas" person.

Best used for making your ideas pay well.

Essential oils or scented candles can be very advantageous, particularly if nothing is happening in your life. Try eucalyptus, orange, mint, rosemary or pine.

Best used for creating activity in your career especially if you need to be noticed.

Green and red color schemes in the fame area have a very positive effect. Try to make sure your furnishings feature some of these colors if painting the walls seems over the top.

Best used for creating steady, positive growth in your reputation.

Pictures are very influential. If you want your career to take off, it would be appropriate to hang pictures or photos that feature a balloon rising into the air, or a flock of birds flying, or even a rocket speeding through the atmosphere.

Best used for propelling your career forward.

A red or green lava lamp and, in fact, all lights belong to the fire element. When placed and lit in the fame area, a lamp will keep activity flowing smoothly.

Best used for creating steady movement in your career.

A lava lamp will help everything go smoothly, particularly in your work life, and will also give you inspiration.

131

Fashion, clothes and feng shui

The shades and shapes that are "in" influence everybody. Clothes wear us—we don't wear them—and they affect how we feel and behave. If you are wearing a tight suit you won't be able to flop down on a couch in the way you would if you were wearing jeans and a sweater. Where and how we keep our clothes, and what we choose to wear can have a subtle influence on our lives.

- Keeping your clothes in a separate dressing room will mean it is easier to keep your bedroom fresh and tidy. While you are sleeping you are healing so your bedroom should be clutter free. Your last and first waking thoughts will then be restful rather than "I must put those things away." Otherwise, you will create immediate stress that is debilitating to your health. If you wake up feeling happy with your clutter-free environment, over a long period of time it will gradually strengthen your health by promoting more restful sleep and waking moments.

- Less is more, so borrow or rent clothes for a formal wedding or special occasion rather than fill your closet with something that you will only wear once in a blue moon. This applies to evening wear and extravagant clothes that you would wear infrequently.

- If you want to stop working so hard and concentrate on other facets of your life, wear floppier clothes and longer lengths. This will make you more relaxed and undisciplined. It is not by chance that we wear casual clothes on the weekend when we are resting or

Colors and feng shui

When colors that are complementary come into fashion, it is a good sign of harmony, peace and tolerance. Complementary colors are blue and gold (water and metal), green and red (tree and fire), blue and white (water and metal), and brown and red (earth and fire).

But when clashing colors are "in," like gray and red (metal and fire) or blue and red (water and fire), it indicates that there is a bigger divide growing between the wealthy and the poor, or between political groups and suggests general discord.

GREEN tends to mean that we will all become more interested in outdoor activities. This color also promotes international travel.

PINK is a soft romantic color. When it is in style we will generally be concentrating on the more feminine aspects of life.

GRAY can bring depression. When it comes into fashion, it can indicate the advent of a downturn in the economy.

BLUE as a color in vogue indicates that society is becoming more conservative, truthful and steady in attitude.

BROWN is a very grounding, conservative, steady color. It represents a solidifying of the economy—safe and sure but not very capable of change.

spending money, and wear more formal clothes like suits during the week when we are earning. If you work in a job that doesn't allow you to dress casually, you could just add a scarf or a humorous tie.

- If you want to make a lot of money and be more organized, wear a suit. When we are dressed this way our body movements become more controlled, upright and efficient, which in turn makes our minds more efficient.

- If you are a woman and want to influence people and attract money, wear a short skirt—not ridiculously short but on the knee or a couple of inches above.

How shoes affect our lives

- Kitten heels are difficult to keep your balance in. They are low so they indicate insecurity and a weakening of the economy.

- Square-toed shoes are balanced and more powerful because they give your feet plenty of room. They indicate a time of commercial growth and confidence.

- Shoes with pointed toes pressurize and squeeze the feet. They represent lack of movement and a conservative, rigid and controlled aspect. It is not a good sign for the economy when they are in style.

- Stiletto heels are sexy, provocative and a bit daring. They are a good sign for the economy but indicate that the pinnacle of the market is near.

- Platform shoes mean a time of plenty and growth in a steady, safe fashion. But they also suggest that we have nearly reached the top of the market.

- When there are no set styles, then people have lost their way; there are many different levels of society and many different things going on. This indicates a certain breakdown of society.

- When artificial fur and feathers are fashionable, they indicate a weak and delicately exotic aspect to life. They are generally short-lived. Wearing predatory animal prints will in turn transform us into more predatory creatures.

ORANGE is the color of healing. People who wear it tend to be followers and healers. It is rarely fashionable for long because we cannot keep up with the vibration that orange generates. It adds a lot of positive warmth to society.

RED brings rapid growth and is one of the most auspicious colors for the Chinese. The vibrant color of life, red represents growth and a state of happiness.

PURPLE is the color of the visionary. It is the color that the church adopted because it is the color of the dreamer, the martyr and of pure (not necessarily physical) love.

BLACK is associated with power. It is a color that is closely linked with money, especially when complemented with gold, so these colors mean financial success for the economy.

YELLOW, when related to fashion, means that everyone is tending to focus more on the intellect.

WHITE indicates a fresh start but possibly a lack of focus for the economy as a whole.

Protecting your home

Our home is our castle; it is our sanctuary from the world and a place where we can relax and recover from the stresses of modern life. This chapter is full of feng shui cures that you can use to keep your home safe and protected.

A bagua mirror is one of the most powerful and protective cures available. It consists of a small, round mirror that may be concave (to diminish and turn upside down approaching foes), flat (for general purposes) or convex (which is more far reaching). The mirror may be set inside an octagonal frame. This is a very powerful shape with the trigrams of the I Ching inscribed around it in either the pre- or post-heaven sequence. It is usually red, gold and green and its inscriptions represent everything in heaven and on earth and all the transformations. A bagua mirror draws energy towards it and is considered to have the power to preserve against misfortune and assure future prosperity.

Wearing a mayan ball whenever you want to deflect negative energy that may be coming towards you is a very powerful cure.

If you have anything threatening your home, perhaps unpleasant neighbors, a road pointing towards your house, a power station or if you are going on vacation and you want to protect your home, simply hang a bagua mirror so that the mirror part shines towards the negativity.

Best used for strong protection against invisible threats.

Mayan balls and all shiny silver objects deflect negative energy. When I am teaching, I always wear a mayan ball as a pendant over my heart. This is because it is almost impossible to keep everyone happy all the time. I will be going too fast for some people and too slowly for others, which will make me vulnerable to psychological attack. We've all experienced this. You may have walked into a room and someone didn't like the color of your hair or what you were wearing. A mayan ball helps to deflect this form of negative energy. If you have a difficult meeting ahead of you or you are going on a long journey or if you have moved in a direction that has upset your personal chi, wear a mayan ball to protect you personally.

Best used for protecting an individual or a car (see page 126).

Carved or porcelain fu dogs will protect your home if you place them on either side of a doorway or window.

A dog coming into your life indicates future prosperity. This is specially true if a strange dog comes and finds you. The dog is valued for his fidelity. The Chinese believe the Pekinese is a remarkably intelligent dog that can do all manner of tricks, from leading horses to holding a torch in its mouth to light the way for its imperial master. Pekineses are fiercely loyal and protective and are the model for the fu (or lion) dog. The fu dog has a trifid tail, a short thick body, big fierce eyes, an open snarling mouth and a beautifully curled mane. Under the paw of the female dog is a cub or engraved ball symbolically containing all that we hold dear in the way of people, compassion, kindness, virtue and love. The male dog has another ball beneath his paw, which contains all our material possessions. Fu dogs should be positioned on either side of an entrance or in a window so they can see all who approach. The balls they hold should be on the inside.

Best used for protecting a property.

The rooster belongs to the fire element and can balance an unstable, dangerous and volatile sha that creates all-consuming fires. If you have a property that is inclined to fire (perhaps it has a history of fire), keep a picture or a figurine of a rooster within the house, either in the kitchen or in the hall. The rooster is also very protective and benevolent to his family. He is admired as a courageous bird because he summons the hens to eat any food he finds. He symbolizes male vigor and reliability, because he always crows at dawn. A crowing cock represents achievement and fame.

Best used for protecting against fire.

Transcendental cure

To protect your property, first of all raise your right arm from the elbow so that your fingers point to the sky. Then visualize an impenetrable shield coming down over the front of the house. At the same time, lower and straighten your arm so that your fingers are pointing directly in front of you at elbow height. Make a rapid "shhh" noise. Repeat this sequence five more times while paying attention to the roof, foundations and the four walls. At the same time visualize an impregnable wall that no one can penetrate surrounding your home. Finally say the mantra *Om manee padme hum* nine times.

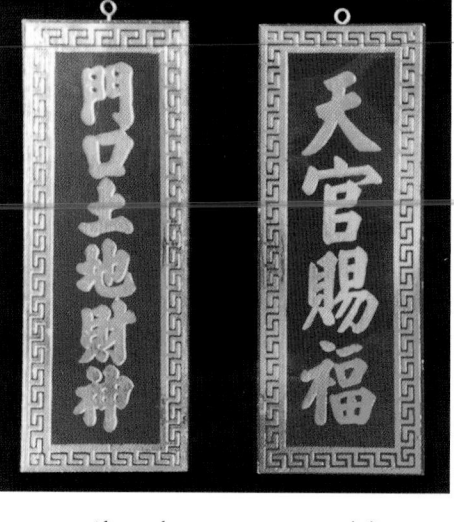

Always hang door guardians in pairs, one on either side of a doorway.

Door guardians in the shape of scrolls or plaques have been used to protect and bless a house or portal since before the Ming Dynasty, which ruled from 1368 to 1664. According to ancient custom, one guardian would be placed on the right side or on both sides of an entrance to guard against the loss of health and money. The energies of these plaques are derived from Cheng Lun who is known as Heng (the Snorter). He has magical powers that were given to him by a magician called Tu O. When he blew air from his nose it made the sound of a terrible bell and two columns of light shot from his nostrils like death rays and destroyed his foes. The other plaque represents Chen Chi who is known as Ha (the Blower). The same magician gave him the power to exhale clouds of toxic yellow gas. The story goes that Heng and Ha once fought against each other—chemical warfare against the death ray! Ha with his poisonous gas was the dominant aggressor until he was wounded and killed by conventional weapons of the time. But the success of Heng, the victor, was short-lived because he was also destroyed by an ox-spirit that spat a bezoar stone into his face. Using these plaques is supposed to summon the spirits of these two warriors to protect your home. **Best used for protecting against robbery and assault.**

A bottle gourd is an object that is endowed with Taoist magic and is said to contain magic potions. Its figure-of-eight shape is a miniature replica of heaven, earth and eternity. When the bottle is opened, an invisible cloud comes out which can be used to trap demons. It is always on the side of good. **Best used for improving the atmosphere and making the environment safe.**

Talismans, charms and amulets are often made of yellow paper with a message or spell written on them in blood. Traditionally, they were written to evil spirits to prevent them from harming the bearer of the amulet. The writing was "ghost script" which is a form of writing that looks similar to Chinese characters but is only fully accessible to Taoist adepts. These talismans or amulets would either be worn about the person over the breast, back or on the shoulder, or hung within a building or boat to protect it. All charms should be replaced on New Year's Day.

There are thousands of different types of amulets or talismans to suit different circumstances. They can be written on a variety of different shapes and shades of paper, but they are usually in the form of a narrow rectangular shape and are hung portrait style. But they may be octagonal, round, triangular or star-shaped. Talismans range from ones that are hung over pigsties to protect against disease to swallow-ashes charms (which are

Bottle gourds are a protective feng shui cure that can be placed in any of the bagua areas of your home.

burned, mixed with water and drunk as medicine). These are usually given when there is illness or threat of illness in the family. There are other talismans for the protection of houses and graves. You may also find an illuminating demon charm which is usually worn on a cord around the neck.

Best used for all manner of protection.

Two bamboo flutes can be used as a cure to transform aggression into peace. They should be hung on red ribbon at a 30-degree angle from a large beam. As a transcendental cure they reduce any divisive influences. Bamboo flutes can also be hung near a front door from red ribbon as a protective measure.

Best used for transforming aggression into peace.

The 100 family charm comprises coins stuck on to a red background and is hung above the marital bed. Traditionally, when a couple have a party, all their friends donate 100 different coins between them. This charm ensures that the couple's child will have a healthy, wealthy and happy life.

Best used for protecting a child and ensuring his luck.

Hang brass or copper coins in the shape of a sword from a red cord or ribbon over the marital bed.

Brass or copper coins fashioned into the shape of a sword were traditionally used to hang over the head of a bed. This was in the belief that the monarchs who reigned when the coins were made would keep away ghosts and evil spirits and thus prevent damage to the mind and any head disorders. These coins are a requisite in rooms or houses where people have committed suicide or have suffered a violent death. They are also used by sick people to hasten recovery, and they can be hung over the cots of newborn babies to guard them in their most vulnerable years.

Best used for protecting health.

A necklace of peach stones or peach wood is regarded as a powerful antidote against evil spirits. You may have observed that priests sometimes wear a string of carved peach stones, which look like a rosary. Peach-stone necklaces can be buried in the foundations of buildings or bridges or worn by a person to bring solidarity, strength and protection.

Best used for protection in healing or spiritual work.

Installing black fish in a fish tank or aquarium will protect all aspects of your health and work.

Black fish have very protective attributes. If a fish dies for no obvious reason like insufficient food, poor water or lack of oxygen, it is believed that the dead fish has absorbed some bad luck that was coming your way. Black fish are specially valued for protecting people's health and careers. Get black fish in pairs as this makes them stronger. **Best used for protecting health and career.**

Firecrackers are often used when cleansing a house. A cheap and easy alternative is to put pieces of bamboo (about 3 inches long) into a fire. These will explode with a loud cracking noise which reverberates through the house, cleansing even the deepest corners and clearing any negativity with their vibration. (Always use a fire guard to protect against any sparks.)
Best used for cleansing after an unwelcome visitor has left.

139

Further information

Sarah Shurety teaches all facets of feng shui including Classical Landscape Form School, The Four Pillars of Destiny, Space Cleansing, The Compass School, Nine Star Ki and Feng Shui for Gardens from introductory to advanced levels.

Please contact The Feng Shui Company for information about personal, telephone or postal consultations for your home or business by Sarah Shurety or one of our qualified consultants.

The Feng Shui Company
Ballard House
37 Norway Street
Greenwich
London SE10 9DD
UK

tel/fax: +44 7000 781901

Information about feng shui seminars and consultations in the US can be obtained from the following websites:

www.amfengshui.com
www.earthlink.net
www. fengshuidirectory.com
www.worldoffengshui.com
wsfs.com/consulting.htm

For information on interior designers and architects qualified to practice feng shui contact the American Society of Interior Designers (ASID) at the following website:

www. asid.org

Feng shui cures

The cures mentioned in this book are available through The Lucky Feng Shui Company Ltd. These include a wide range of wind chimes, mayan balls, purifying incense, bagua mirrors, flutes and fountains. Books are also available. Please telephone for a free catalogue or send an s.a.e. to:

The Lucky Feng Shui Company Ltd
Sunshine Cottage
Chedzoy
Somerset TA7 8RW
UK

tel/fax: +44 7000 781901

Other suppliers of feng shui cures in the US include:

Carol Meltzer
tel: (212) 598 4848

Tin Sun Metaphysics
tel: (212) 285 0522

Index

Acknowledgments

Very special thanks are extended to Mandarin Arts Ltd and Typhoon Ltd, who kindly loaned props for the photographs specially taken for this book, and to Coach of Sloane Street, London, for the loan of handbags and leather goods.

The publishers and author would also like to thank the following for their kind permission to reproduce these photographs.

26 Elizabeth Whiting Associates; 29 Robert Harding/IPC Magazines/Country Homes and Interiors/Andreas von Einsiedel; 43 S & O Mathews; 45 Elizabeth Whiting Associates/Rodney Hyett; 52 Elizabeth Whiting Associates/Andreas von Einsiedel; 60 S & O Mathews; 83 top Photomax; 83 bottom Robert Harding/IPC Magazines/Homes and Ideas/Dominic Blackmore; 99 Robert Harding/IPC Magazines/Homes and Gardens/Jan Baldwin; 101 Clive Nichols/designer: Jill Billington; 108 top from *The Lives of the Saints* (Random House UK Ltd); 115 bottom S & O Mathews; 118 bottom Elizabeth Whiting Associates/Tania Midgley; 121 Robert Harding/IPC Magazines/Homes and Interiors/Nic Barlow; 122 Robert Harding/IPC Magazines/Homes and Gardens/Kiloran Howard; 123 Elizabeth Whiting Associates/Andreas von Einsiedel; 124 Elizabeth Whiting Associates/Tim Imrie; 139 Photomax.

The following photographs were supplied by The Lucky Feng Shui Company Ltd: 88–91 (glass animals), 134, 136 by Q.P.C., Photography, Unit 17, Acorn Business Centre, Livingstone Way, Taunton, Somerset; 115 top and 125 bottom by CLIQ Studio, 9 Portman Crescent, North Petherton, Somerset.